国家哲学社会科学项目英语专业内容依托课程改革研究成果
第六届国家级优秀教学成果奖
辽宁省优秀教学成果一等奖

21世纪CBI内容依托系列英语教材

Understanding the U.K. Physical and Human Geography

英国国情
英国自然人文地理

（第2版）

常俊跃 赵秀艳 赵永青 主编

图书在版编目(CIP)数据

英国国情：英国自然人文地理/常俊跃，赵秀艳，赵永青主编. —2版. —北京：北京大学出版社，2016.9
（21世纪CBI内容依托系列英语教材）
ISBN 978-7-301-27081-3

Ⅰ. ①英… Ⅱ. ①常… ②赵… ③赵… Ⅲ. ①英语—高等学校—教材 ②自然地理学—英国 ③人文地理学—英国 Ⅳ. ① H319.4:P ② H319.4:K

中国版本图书馆CIP数据核字(2016) 第084034号

书　　名	英国国情：英国自然人文地理（第2版） YINGGUO GUOQING:YINGGUO ZIRAN RENWEN DILI
著作责任者	常俊跃　赵秀艳　赵永青　主编
责任编辑	初艳红
标准书号	ISBN 978-7-301-27081-3
出版发行	北京大学出版社
地　　址	北京市海淀区成府路205号　100871
网　　址	http://www.pup.cn　　新浪微博：@北京大学出版社
电子邮箱	编辑部 pupwaiwen@pup.cn　总编室 zpup@pup.cn
电　　话	邮购部 62752015　发行部 62750672　编辑部 62759634
印 刷 者	北京虎彩文化传播有限公司
经 销 者	新华书店
	787毫米×1098毫米　16开本　12.5印张　250千字 2010年1月第1版 2016年9月第2版　2025年2月第3次印刷
定　　价	39.00元

未经许可，不得以任何方式复制或抄袭本书之部分或全部内容。
版权所有，侵权必究
举报电话：010-62752024　电子邮箱：fd@pup.cn
图书如有印装质量问题，请与出版部联系，电话：010-62756370

编 委 会

本书主编
常俊跃　赵秀艳　赵永青

本书编校主要参与者
Alastair Clark　夏　洋　李莉莉　胡毓敏　曲小岑　刘　翔

对本项目教材开发有贡献的其他教师
宋　杰　傅　琼　刘晓菓　霍跃红　高璐璐
黄洁芳　姚　璐　吕春媚　李文萍　范丽雅

前　言

随着我国英语教育的快速发展,英语专业长期贯彻的"以技能为导向"的课程建设理念及教学理念已经难以满足社会的需要。专家教师们密切关注的现行英语专业教育大、中、小学英语教学脱节,语言、内容教学割裂,单纯语言技能训练过多,专业内容课程不足,学科内容课程系统性差,高、低年级内容课程安排失衡及其导致的学生知识面偏窄、知识结构欠缺、思辨能力偏弱、综合素质发展不充分等问题日益凸显。

针对上述问题,大连外国语大学英语专业在内容与语言融合教学理念的指导下确定了如下改革思路:

(一) 更新语言教学理念,改革英语专业教育的课程结构。改变传统单一的语言技能课程模式,实现内容课程与语言课程的融合,扩展学生的知识面,提高学生的语言技能。

(二) 开发课程自身潜力,同步提高专业知识和语言技能。课程同时关注内容和语言,把内容教学和语言教学有机结合。以英语为媒介,系统教授专业内容;以专业内容为依托,在使用语言过程中提高语言技能,扩展学生的知识面,提高思辨能力。

(三) 改革教学方法,全面提高语言技能和综合素质。依靠内容依托教学在方法上的灵活性,通过问题驱动、输出驱动等方法调动学生主动学习,把启发式、任务式、讨论式、结对子、小组活动、课堂展示、多媒体手段等行之有效的活动与学科内容教学有机结合,提高学生的语言技能,激发学生的兴趣,培养学生的自主性和创造性,提升思辨能力和综合素质。

本项改革突破了我国英语专业英语教学大纲规定的课程结构,改变了英语专业通过开设单纯的听、说、读、写、译语言技能课程提高学生语言技能的传统课程建设理念,对英语课程及教学方法进行了创新性的改革。首创了具有我国特色的英语专业内容与语言融合的课程体系;开发了适合英语专业的内容与语言融合的课程;以英语为媒介,比较系统地教授专业内容;以内容为依托,全面发展学生的语言技能;扩展学生的知识面,提高学生的综合素质,以崭新的途径实现英语专业教育的总体培养目标。

经过十年的实验探索,改革取得了鼓舞人心的结果。

(一) 构建了英语专业内容与语言融合教学的课程体系。课程包括美国历史文化、美国自然人文地理、美国社会文化、英国历史文化、英国自然人文地理、英国社会文化、澳新加社会文化、欧洲文化、中国文化、跨文化交际、《圣经》与文化、希腊罗马神话、综合英语(美国文学经典作品)、综合英语(英国文学经典作品)、综合英语(世界文学经典作品)、综合英语(西方思想经典)、英语视听说(美国社会文化经典电影)、英语视听说(英国社会文化经典电影)、英语视听说(环球资讯)、英语视听说(专题资讯)、英语短篇小说、英语长篇小说、英语散文、英语诗歌、英语戏剧、英语词汇学、英语语言学、语言与社会、语言与文化、语言与语用等。这些课程依托专业知识内容训练学生综合运用语言的能力,扩展学生的知识面,提高学生的多元文化意识,提升学生的综合素质。

(二)系统开发了相关国家的史、地、社会文化以及跨文化交际课程资源。在内容与语言融合教学理念的指导下,开发了上述课程的资源。开发的教材改变了传统的组织模式,系统组织了教学内容,设计了新颖的栏目板块,设计的活动也丰富多样,实践教学中受到了学生的广泛欢迎。此外还开发了开设课程所需要的教学课件等。在北京大学出版社、华中科技大学出版社、北京师范大学出版社的支持下,系列教材已经陆续出版。

(三)牵动了教学手段和教学方法的改革,取得了突出的教学效果。在内容与语言融合教学理念的指导下,教师的教学理念、教学方法、教学手段得到更新。通过问题驱动、输出驱动等活动调动学生主动学习,把启发式、任务式、讨论式、结对子、小组活动、课堂展示、多媒体手段等行之有效的活动与学科内容教学有机结合,激发学生的兴趣,培养学生的自主性和创造性,提高学生的语言技能,提升思辨能力和综合素质。曾有专家、教师担心取消、减少语言技能课程会对学生的语言技能发展产生消极影响。实验数据证明,内容与语言融合教学不仅没有对学生的语言技能发展和语言知识的学习产生消极影响,而且还产生了多方面的积极影响,对专业知识的学习也产生了巨大的积极影响。

(四)提高了教师的科研意识和科研水平,取得了丰硕的教研成果。开展改革以来,团队对内容与语言融合教学问题进行了系列研究,活跃了整个教学单位的科研气氛,科研意识和科研水平也得到很大提高。课题组已经撰写研究论文60多篇,撰写博士论文3篇,在国内外学术期刊发表研究论文40多篇,撰写专著2部。

教学改革开展以来,每次成果发布都引起强烈反响。在第三届中国外语教学法国际研讨会上,与会的知名外语教育专家戴炜栋教授等对这项改革给予关注,博士生导师蔡基刚教授认为本项研究"具有导向性作用"。在第二届全国英语专业院系主任高级论坛上,研究成果得到知名专家、博士生导师王守仁教授和与会专家教授的高度评价。在中国英语教学研究会年会上,成果再次引起与会专家的强烈反响,博士生导师石坚教授等给予了高度评价。本项改革的系列成果两次获得大连外国语大学教学研究成果一等奖,两次获得辽宁省优秀教学成果奖一等奖,一次获得国家教学成果奖。目前,该项改革成果已经在全国英语专业教育领域引起广泛关注。它触及了英语专业的教学大纲,影响了课程建设的理念,引领了英语专业的教学改革,改善了教学实践,必将对未来英语专业教育的发展产生积极影响。

《英国国情:英国自然人文地理》是英语专业内容依托课程体系改革与创新这项国家级教学成果的重要组成部分,是英语专业核心必修课程基础英语所使用的教材。教材针对的学生群体是具有中学英语基础的大学生,适用于英语专业一、二年级学生,也适用于具有中学英语基础的非英语专业学生和英语爱好者学习。总体来看,本教材具备以下主要特色:

(一)遵循了全新的教学理念

经过几十年的快速发展,我国的英语教学已经出现了翻天覆地的变化。今天的英语学习者不再满足只是单词、语法、句型等等英语语言知识的学习,他们更希望读到地道的英语,在享受英语阅读乐趣的同时又能增长知识、开阔视野、了解英语国家,进而更好地运用英语与英语国家人民进行交流。本教材改变了"为学语言而学语言"的传统教材建设理念,在具有时代特色且被证明行之有效的内容依托教学理论指导下,改变了片面关注语言知识和语言技能、忽视内容学习的做法。它依托学生密切关注的英国地理文化知识,结合英国自然人文知识内容组织学生进行语言交际活动,在语言交流中学习有意义的知识内容,既训练语言技能,也丰富相关知识,起到的是一箭双雕的作用。

(二)涉及了系统的地理内容

《英国国情:英国自然人文地理》是一本系统关注英国自然地理和人文地理的教材。全书共分15个单元,从英格兰、苏格兰、威尔士及北爱尔兰对英国的自然和人文进行介绍;其中英格兰被分成西南部、东南部、伦敦、东部、中东部、中西部、西北部、约克郡-亨伯以及东北部9个区域。读者从中可以了解到英国诸郡及重要城市,领略英国的山川河湖以及国家公园的美景;除此之外,读者还可以了解到英国的人文知识:传奇的历史、有趣的传说、伟大的人物、奇异的遗址、著名的大学等等。

(三)引进了真实的教学材料

英语教材是英语学习者英语语言输入和相关知识输入的重要渠道。本教材大量使用真实、地道的语言材料,为学生提供了高质量的语言输入。此外,为了使课文内容更加充实生动,易于学生理解接受,编者在课文中穿插了大量的插图、表格、照片等真实的视觉材料。表现手段活泼,形式多种多样,效果生动直观。让读者身临其境,感同身受。

(四)设计了新颖的教材板块

本教材每一单元的主体内容均包括 Before You Read、Start to Read、After You Read 和 Read More 四大板块,也就是课前热身、课文正文、课后练习和辅助阅读。除此之外有专有名词列表和娱乐园地,教材的最后还有附录内容。课前热身包括启发性的问题或准备活动;课文正文介绍英国重要的自然和人文地理知识并突出显示了语汇学习重点;课后练习关注英国地理知识的学习和英语语言的学习;辅助阅读内容对课文正文进行补充,为学有余力的读者提供更多更详细的内容;专有名词列表为读者省去了查阅英国地理专有名词的麻烦;娱乐园地介绍的相关网址、电影、书籍、歌曲等可供读者选择自己感兴趣的内容对英国自然人文地理进行多角度的探索;附录内容介绍了英格兰、苏格兰、威尔士以及北爱尔兰的守护神、象征物、国花、国旗、国歌等。教材不仅在结构上确立了学生的主体地位,而且系统的安排也方便教师借助教材有条不紊地开展教学活动。

(五)提供了多样的训练活动

为了培养学生的语言技能和综合素质,本教材在保证英国地理知识体系完整的前提下,在关注英语语言知识训练和相关知识内容传授的基础上精心设计了生动多样的综合训练活动,如课堂展示、小组讨论、故事接龙、对比写作等等。教材在每一单元都精心设计了英语词汇、地理知识等练习。同时,设计出与英国地理相关的、学生参与度极高的课堂和课外活动。多样化的活动打破了传统教材单调的训练程式,帮助教师设置真实的语言运用情境,组织富于挑战性的、具有意义的语言实践活动。它们改变了教师单纯灌输、学生被动接受的教学方式,促使学生积极思考、提问、探索、发现、批判,培养自主获得知识、发现问题和解决问题的能力。

(六)推荐了经典的学习材料

教材的另一特色在于它对教学内容的延伸和拓展。在每个单元的最后,编者向学生推荐经典的书目、影视作品、名诗欣赏以及英文歌曲等学习资料,这不仅有益于学生开阔视野,也使教材具有了弹性和开放性,方便不同院校不同水平学生的使用。

(七)引进了先进的数码技术

采用"互联网+"技术,实现从纸质资源到立体化多媒体资源的立体呈现,学习者可利用移动设备上的二维码扫描软件在线阅读相关内容和收听相关录音。

本教材是我国英语专业综合英语课程改革的一项探索,凝聚了全体编写人员的艰苦努力。然而由于水平所限,还存在疏漏和不足,希望使用本教材的老师和同学们能为我们提出意见和建议。您的指导和建议将是我们提高的动力。

编者

2016年5月

于大连外国语大学

目录

Unit 1　Panoramic View of the UK / 1
　　Text A　View of the UK / 2
　　Text B　Names about the UK / 7
　　Text C　Britain and Ireland / 8

Unit 2　A Survey of England / 13
　　Text A　View of England / 14
　　Text B　Climate in England / 19

Unit 3　South West England / 25
　　Text A　View of South West / 26
　　Text B　The Origin of Bath / 31
　　Text C　Stonehenge / 33

Unit 4　South East England / 37
　　Text A　View of South East England / 38
　　Text B　Oxford University / 44
　　Text C　On *The Canterbury Tales* / 45

Unit 5　London / 50
　　Text A　Greater London and the City of London / 51
　　Text B　Landmarks in London / 53
　　Text C　More Landmarks / 57

Unit 6　The East of England / 63
　　Text A　View of the East of England / 64
　　Text B　New Stone Installed with China's Best-known Poem / 70

Unit 7　East Midlands / 74
　　Text A　View of East Midlands / 75
　　Text B　Heroes in Nottinghamshire / 81

Unit 8 West Midlands / 87
   Text A   View of West Midlands / 88
   Text B   Stratford-Upon-Avon / 94

Unit 9 North West England / 99
   Text A   View of North West England / 100
   Text B   The Beatles / 106

Unit 10 Yorkshire and the Humber / 111
   Text A   View of Yorkshire and the Humber / 112
   Text B   Bradford / 117

Unit 11 North East England / 122
   Text A   View of North East England / 123
   Text B   Hadrian's Wall / 129

Unit 12 Scotland / 134
   Text A   View of Scotland / 135
   Text B   Loch Ness / 144
   Text C   Thistle: Scotland's National Flower / 145

Unit 13 Wales / 151
   Text A   View of Wales / 152
   Text B   Legends of Wales / 158

Unit 14 Northern Ireland / 162
   Text A   View of Northern Ireland / 163
   Text B   Legend of Giant's Causeway / 170
   Text C   St. Patrick's Day / 170

Unit 15 Review of the UK / 175
   Text A   Review of England and Scotland / 176
   Text B   Review of Wales / 182
   Text C   Review of Northern Ireland / 183

Appendixes
   Appendix 1   Symbols of Constituent Countries of the UK / 186
   Appendix 2   National Flags / 187

重点参考书目和网站 / 188

Unit 1
Panoramic View of the UK

> When people say England, they sometimes mean Great Britain, sometimes the United Kingdom, sometimes the British Isles, but never England.
>
> — George Mikes

Unit Goals

- To have a general idea of the geography of the UK
- To be familiar with the geographical terms about the UK
- To be able to introduce the location and composition of the UK
- To be able to describe the general landscape of the UK
- To be able to make a comparison between the UK and the USA
- To be able to use articles more skillfully

 ### Before You Read

1. How large is the UK compared with the USA? Which of the following shows the possible proportion?

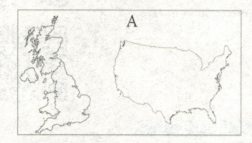

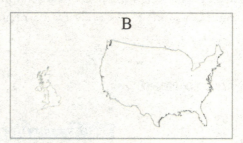

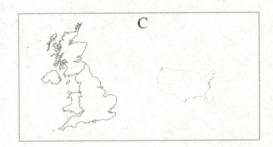
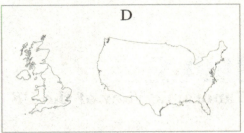

2. Where is the UK? Tick (√) the neighboring countries and the neighbouring seas.

Countries	√	Oceans	√
China		the Pacific	
Belgium		the Atlantic	
France		the Indian	
Ireland		the Arctic	
Germany		the North Sea	
Denmark		the Irish Sea	
Netherlands		the English Channel	

3. What are the four countries that make up the UK? England, _____, _____, and _____.
4. Is the UK mountainous or flat?
5. Have you ever heard of Lock Ness which is famous for a monster? Where is it in the UK?
6. **Group Work**: Form groups of three or four students. Try to find, on the Internet or in the library, more general information about the UK, which interests you most. Get ready for a 5-minute presentation in class.

Start to Read

Text A   View of the UK

Location and Composition

The official title of the UK is the *United Kingdom of Great Britain and*

Northern Ireland. It is an island nation in Western Europe just off the coast of France. The mainland areas lie between latitudes 49°N and 59°N and longitudes 8°W to 2°E. The UK lies between the North Atlantic Ocean and the North Sea, and comes within 35 km (22 miles) of the northwest coast of France, from which it is separated by

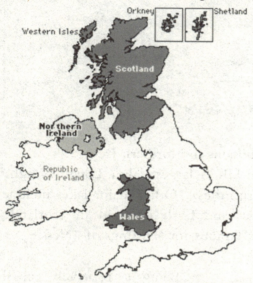

the English Channel. Northern Ireland shares a 360 km international land boundary with the Republic of Ireland. The Channel Tunnel bored beneath the English Channel, now links the UK with France.

 The UK is made up of several islands: Great Britain (the formerly separate realms of England and Scotland, and the principality of Wales), Northern Ireland (also known as Ulster), and **numerous** smaller islands including the Isle of Wight, Anglesey, and the Scilly, Orkney, Shetland, and Hebrides. The only land border connecting the UK to another country is between Northern Ireland and the Republic of Ireland. The UK is bordered by four seas: to the south by the English Channel, which separates it from continental Europe; to the east by the North Sea; to the west by the Irish Sea and the Atlantic Ocean.

Landscape

 The UK has a total area of approximately 245,000 km^2, almost a quarter of a million square kilometers. Its landscape is very varied, **ranging from** the Grampian Mountains of Scotland **to** the lowland fens of England, which are at or below sea level in places.

Scotland and Wales are the most mountainous parts of the UK. A ridge of hills, the Pennines, runs down the centre of northern England. Many coastal areas are low-lying, especially in the east and south of England. These include the wetlands of the Somerset levels, which regularly flood during heavy rain.

Most of the UK is made up of gently rolling hills with isolated areas of high ground such as Dartmoor in the southwest of England or the Mourne Mountains in Northern Ireland.

Northern Ireland is also home to the UK's largest lake, Lough Neagh, which covers an area of 396 sq. km (153 sq miles). Other major lakes include Windermere in the English Lake District and Loch Lomond in Scotland. Another of Scotland's lakes, Loch Ness is famous for sightings of "Nessie", a mythical monster!

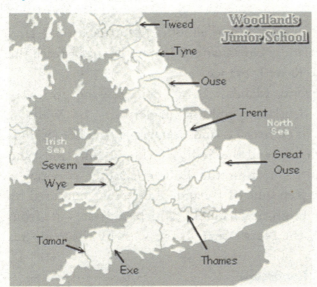

Being a relatively small Island, the UK's rivers are not very long. The Severn, its longest river, is just 354 km in length, beginning in Wales and entering the Atlantic Ocean near Bristol in England. Other major rivers include the Thames, which flows through Oxford and London, and the Trent and Mersey rivers, which drain rainfall from large areas of central England.

After You Read

Knowledge Focus

1. **Fill in the blanks according to the geographical knowledge you have learned in the text above.**
   (1) The UK is an island nation in _____ Europe just off the coast of _____.
   (2) The UK is separated from France by the _____.
   (3) The UK is mainly made up of England, Scotland, _____, and _____.
   (4) The longest river in the UK is _____, which begins in _____.
   (5) _____, a lake in Scotland, is famous for sightings of a mythical monster.
   (6) The largest lake in the UK is _____, and it is located in _____.
   (7) A ridge of hills, _____, called the "backbone of England", runs down the center of Northern England.
   (8) _____, one of the major rivers in the UK, flows through Oxford and London.

2. **Write T in the brackets if the statement is true and write F if it is false.**
   (1) The official title of the UK is the *United Kingdom of Great Britain and Ireland*. ( )
   (2) The Channel Tunnel bored beneath the North Sea links the UK with France. ( )
   (3) The only land border connecting the UK to another country is between Northern Ireland and the Republic of Ireland. ( )
   (4) The UK is bordered by the North Sea to the East. ( )
   (5) Scotland and England are the most mountainous parts of the UK. ( )
   (6) Lough Neagh, the largest lake in the UK is located in Wales. ( )
   (7) Nessie is an animal living in Lock Ness in Scotland. ( )
   (8) There are many rivers in the UK, such as the Severn and the Thames. ( )

3. **Discuss the following questions with your partner.**
   (1) What is the official title of the UK?
   (2) Where is the UK?
   (3) What geographical relationship does the UK have with Ireland?
   (4) What tunnel links the UK and France? And where is it?
   (5) What are the capital cities of the four countries in the UK?

Language Focus

1. **Fill in the blanks with the proper form of the phrases below.**

be home to	link...with	be famous for
range from...to	be made up of	share...with

   (1) The UK _____ several islands.
   (2) The UK's landscape is very varied, _____ the Grampian Mountains of Scotland _____ the lowland fens of England.

(3) Another of Scotland's lakes, Loch Ness _____ sightings of "Nessie", a mythical monster!

(4) Northern Ireland _____ a 360 km international land boundary _____ the Republic of Ireland.

(5) The Channel Tunnel bored beneath the English Channel, now _____ the UK _____ France.

(6) Northern Ireland _____ the UK's largest lake, Lough Neagh.

2. **Fill in the blanks with the appropriate form of the words in the brackets.**

(1) Great Britain includes the _____ (former) separate realms of England and Scotland, and the _____ (principal) of Wales.

(2) The low-lying lands in the east and south of England _____ (regular) flood during heavy rain.

(3) The film—*Mee-Shee, The Water Giant*, is about the _____ (myth) monster in Loch Ness.

(4) Dartmoor is an _____ (isolation) area of high ground in the southwest of England.

(5) The Channel Tunnel, _____ (bore) beneath the English Channel, links the UK and France.

(6) The landscape in the UK is varied, _____ (range) from high mountains to lowland fens.

(7) The UK consists of _____ (numerously) small islands.

3. **Fill in the blanks with the proper prepositions and adverbs that collocate with the neighboring words.**

(1) It is an island nation in Western Europe just _____ the coast of France.

(2) The mainland areas lie _____ latitudes 49°N and 59°N and longitudes 8°W to 2°E.

(3) The lowland fens of England are _____ or _____ sea level in places.

(4) The Severn, its longest river, is just 338 km _____ length, beginning _____ Wales and entering the Atlantic Ocean near Bristol in England.

(5) The Channel Tunnel is bored _____ the English Channel.

4. **Correct all the mistakes in using the articles in the following sentences.**

(1) An official title of UK is United Kingdom of Great Britain and Northern Ireland.

(2) It is the island nation in Western Europe just off a coast of France.

(3) The UK lies between North Atlantic Ocean and North Sea.

(4) The Northern Ireland shares the 360 km international land boundary with Republic of the Ireland.

(5) Scotland and Wales are most mountainous part in the UK.

(6) Northern Ireland is also home to UK's largest lake, Lough Neagh. The other lakes include Windermere in English Lake District and Loch Lomond in Scotland.

(7) Severn, its longest river, is just 338 km in the length, beginning in Wales and

entering Atlantic Ocean near the Bristol in England.

Comprehensive Work

1. **Pair Work**: Try to locate the following places on the outline map of the UK with your partner. Don't forget to speak English!

   North Sea
   Atlantic Ocean
   Irish Sea
   Celtic Sea
   English Channel
   England
   Wales
   Scotland
   Northern Ireland
   London
   Edinburgh
   Cardiff
   Belfast
   the Thames
   the Severn
   the Pennines
   the Grampian Mountains
   the Mourne Mountains
   Lough Neagh
   Loch Ness

2. **Solo Work**: Compare the UK with the USA in terms of their size, location, mountains, rivers, landscape, etc. Make a prediction of their future according to their geographical conditions. Write a passage of about 300 words.

Read More

Text B Names about the UK

Read the passage and finish the multiple-choice questions just below the passage.

Did anyone find the **similarities** between the names of "the British Isles", "Great Britain", "the United Kingdom", "England" and "the British Commonwealth"? Strictly speaking, these names all refer to something different. None of them are exactly the same as any of the others.

The British Isles refer to the main islands and several thousand small ones as well, which you can see on the map. Great Britain, or Britain, refers to the larger of the two main islands. But the word "Britain" is often used as a short form for the United Kingdom or you call it the UK.

As for England, it refers simply to the largest of the three countries on the island of Great Britain. The United Kingdom is the name of the state and the official name of the country, which many people popularly refer to as England.

Finally, the British Commonwealth is the usual name for what is left of the British Empire. This change shows the **weakening** of British Empire and the rising of the national liberation movements throughout the world today.

1. According to the passage, we know that _____.
   A. Great Britain has the same meaning as Britain
   B. the United Kingdom has the same meaning as Britain or England
   C. all the names in the first paragraph have the same meaning
   D. all the names refer to England
2. It is clear that the British Isles refer to _____.
   A. Britain, England and the UK
   B. the two main islands and thousands of small ones
   C. three countries and several islands
   D. Great Britain or the United Kingdom
3. Which of the following shows the right relationship between the British Isles (BI), Britain (B) and England (E)?
   A. B>BI>E   B. BI>E>B   C. E>B>BI   D. BI>B>E
4. If you want to write to someone in Edinburgh that lies in Scotland, you can write the address as follows.
   A. Edinburgh, England.
   B. Edinburgh, Great Britain.
   C. Scotland, Edinburgh, England.
   D. Great Britain, Scotland, Edinburgh.

Text C Britain and Ireland

There are 20 blanks in the following passage, and for each blank there are 4 choices marked A, B, C and D at the end of the passage. Circle the answer that best fit into the passage.

What is the difference between the British Isles, Britain, the United Kingdom and England? These terms are so often confused by us.

Unit 1 Panoramic View of the UK

The British Isles is made up of two large islands: One is called Ireland and the other __1__. Britain, or Great Britain, is the larger of these two islands, and it is __2__ into three parts: Scotland, Wales and England.

The United Kingdom is that __3__ of the British Isles ruled over by the Queen. It is made up of Scotland, Wales and England, that is, the __4__ of Britain, and also about one sixth of Ireland, the Northern part. The __5__ of Ireland is **self governing**. The __6__ name of the United Kingdom is __7__ "The United Kingdom of Great Britain and Northern Ireland".

__8__ is larger and richer than Scotland, Wales and Northern Ireland, and has the most __9__ of the United Kingdom, so people often use the __10__ "England" and "English" when they __11__ "Britain" and "British". This sometimes makes the Scots and the Welsh a little __12__. The Scots **in particular** are very __13__ of their separate nationality. The Welsh too do not regard __14__ as English, and have a culture and even a __15__ of their own.

Ireland became part of the United Kingdom in 1801, but for forty years the "Irish __16__" was the greatest headache of the United Kingdom. __17__, Ireland is divided into two: Northern Ireland still __18__ to the United Kingdom and in 1922 the rest of Ireland __19__ to found an Irish Free State, later called Eire and now the Republic of Ireland.

The Republic of Ireland does not regard itself as part of Britain, and is not now even a supporter of the Commonwealth of Nations. Unlike the major Commonwealth countries it did not lift a finger to __20__ British in the Second World War and now wants the whole of Ireland to be a republic.

1. A. Wales   B. Britain   C. England   D. Scotland
2. A. divided   B. cut   C. broken   D. separated
3. A. piece   B. island   C. country   D. part
4. A. south   B. north   C. part   D. whole
5. A. smaller   B. larger   C. rest   D. island
6. A. correct   B. true   C. full   D. complete
7. A. also   B. therefore   C. likely   D. perhaps
8. A. The UK   B. The British isles C. Great Britain   D. England
9. A. colleges   B. officials   C. cities   D. population
10. A. words   B. names   C. spellings   D. pronunciations
11. A. call   B. forget   C. speak   D. write
12. A. angry   B. difficult   C. tired   D. lonely
13. A. proud   B. fond   C. full   D. kind
14. A. it   B. Wales   C. them   D. themselves
15. A. capital   B. language   C. history   D. programmer
16. A. Country   B. Question   C. Disease   D. Republic
17. A. At last   B. So   C. Meanwhile   D. Also

18. A. returns   B. belongs   C. gets   D. speaks
19. A. hoped   B. refused   C. broke away D. used
20. A. feel   B. touch   C. fight   D. help

Proper Nouns

Bristol 布里斯托尔市
Dartmoor 达特姆尔高原
England 英格兰
Great Britain 大不列颠
Hebrides 赫布里底群岛
Lake Windermere 温德米尔湖
Loch Lomond 洛蒙德湖
Loch Ness 尼斯湖
Lough Neagh 内伊湖
Northern Ireland 北爱尔兰
Scotland 苏格兰
the British Isles 不列颠群岛（英伦群岛）
the Channel Tunnel 海峡隧道
the Commonwealth of Nations（又称：the British Commonwealth）英联邦
the English Channel 英吉利海峡
the Irish Sea 爱尔兰海
the Isle of Anglesey 安格尔西岛
the Isle of Scilly 锡利岛
the Isle of Wight 怀特岛
the Lake District 湖区
the Mersey 墨西河
the Mourne Mountains 莫恩山脉
the North Sea 北海
the Orkney Islands 奥克尼岛
the Pennines 奔宁山脉
the Republic of Ireland 爱尔兰共和国
the Severn 塞文河
the Shetland Islands 舍得兰岛
the Somerset Levels 萨默塞特平原
the Thames 泰晤士河
the Trent 特伦特河
the UK (the United Kingdom of Great Britain and Northern Ireland) 英国（大不列颠及北爱尔兰联合王国）
Wales 威尔士

For Fun

Websites to visit

http://www.woodlands-junior.kent.sch.uk/customs/questions/geography.html

　　This is a webpage about the general geography of the UK.

http://edu.sina.com.cn/en/2004-10-25/26874.html

　　This is a webpage on which you can find the answer to and the explanation of Text B and Text C in this unit.

Book to read

National Geographic Traveler: Great Britain by Christopher Somerville

　　Visit every region of this diverse and beguiling land, including the distinctive countries of Scotland and Wales.

This new edition offers the latest information on historic sites, city highlights, scenic drives, walking tours, and more—from London's venerable Westminster Abbey and Shakespeare's scenic hometown of Stratford-Upon-Avon to John Lennon's boyhood home in Liverpool.

Movie to see
King Arthur (2004)

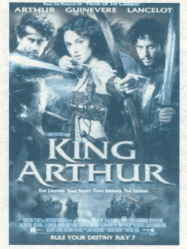

Historians have thought for centuries that King Arthur was only a myth, but the legend was based on a real hero, torn between his private ambitions and his public sense of duty. A reluctant leader, Arthur wishes only to leave Britain and return to the peace and stability of Rome. Before he can head for Rome, one final mission leads him and his Knights of the Round Table, Lancelot, Galahad, Bors, Tristan, and Gawain to the conclusion that when Rome is gone, Britain needs a king—someone not only to defend against the current threat of invading Saxons, but to lead the isle into a new age. Under the guidance of Merlin, a former enemy, and the beautiful, courageous Guinevere by his side, Arthur will have to find the strength within himself to change the course of history.

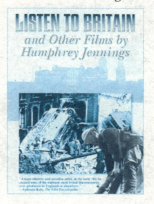

Listen To Britain (1942)

It is a depiction of life in wartime England during the Second World War. Director Humphrey Jennings visits many aspects of civilian life and of the turmoil and privation caused by the war, all without narration.

Song to enjoy

God Save the Queen—the British National Anthem

God save our gracious Queen,
Long live our noble Queen,
God save the Queen!
Send her victorious,
Happy and glorious,
Long to reign over us;
God save the Queen!

O Lord our God arise,
Scatter her enemies
And make them fall;
Confound their politics,
Frustrate their knavish tricks,
On Thee our hopes we fix,
God save us all!

Thy choicest gifts in store
On her be pleased to pour;
Long may she reign;
May she defend our laws,
And ever give us cause
To sing with heart and voice,
God save the Queen!

Not in this land alone,
But be God's mercies known,
From shore to shore!
Lord make the nations see,
That men should brothers be,
And form one family,
The wide world over.

From every latent foe,
From the assassins blow,
God save the Queen!
O'er her thine arm extend,
For Britain's sake defend,
Our mother, prince, and friend,
God save the Queen!

Lord grant that Marshal Wade
May by thy mighty aid
Victory bring.
May he sedition hush,
And like a torrent rush,
Rebellious Scots to crush.
God save the Queen!

Unit 2
A Survey of England

> The stately homes of England! / How beautiful they stand,
> / Amidst their tall ancestral trees, / O'er all the pleasant land!
> — Felicia Hemans

Unit Goals

- To have a general idea of the geography of England
- To be familiar with the geographical terms about England
- To be able to introduce the physical characteristics of England
- To be able to describe the general landscape of England
- To be able to use the passive voice more skillfully

Before You Read

1. Does England mean the UK? Which of the following is the national flag of England?

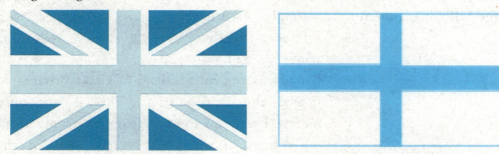

2. Which of the following is the floral emblem of England? Can you match the flowers with their names?

(Daffodil Shamrock Rose Thistle)

3. What is the land in England like? Flat or mountainous?
4. There is an area in England called "the Lake District". Can you guess why?
5. Is the Thames the longest river in England? Is it the longest in the UK?
6. **Group Work**: Form groups of three or four students. Try to find, on the Internet or in the library, more general information about England, for example, its agriculture or economy, which interests you most. Get ready for a 5-minute presentation in class.

Start to Read

Text A　　**View of England**

General Physical Characteristics

England is in northwest Europe and is in the southern part of Great Britain. It is only 35 km from France and is now linked by a tunnel under the English Channel. It is an island country and also part of the United Kingdom. England is the largest country in Great Britain and the UK. It is sometimes, wrongly, used in reference to the whole United Kingdom, the entire island of Great Britain, or indeed the British Isles. This is not only incorrect but can cause **offence** to people from other parts of the UK. Nearly 84% of the population of the UK lives in England, mainly in the major cities and **metropolitan** areas.

England covers over 50,000 square miles (130,439 square kilometers) and is the largest of the countries **comprising** the island of Britain, covering about two-thirds of the island. No place in England is more than 75 miles (120 km) from the sea.

Regions of England

England is divided into nine regions: London, the South East, the South West, the West Midlands, the North West, the North East, Yorkshire and the Humber, the East Midlands and the East of England.

Landscape

The landscape is determined mainly by the different types of rock **underlying** it. In the south, chalk has produced the gently rolling hills of the Downs, while hard granite is the basis for the mountains of the north and the high moorlands of Dartmoor and Exmoor in the southwest.

Much of the land in England is low lying, forming meadowlands and pastures, and less than 10 percent of the area is covered by woodlands. Farmers raise animals or grow crops in the fields.

Upland areas are generally **confined to** northern England: the exceptions are the upland moors of Dartmoor and Exmoor in the southwest.

The landscape of England is more **rugged** in the north and the west. The highest elevations are in Cumbria and the Lake District in the west. The highest point in England is Scafell Pike, 978 m, part of the Cumbrian Mountains in North West England; there are several other high peaks there, too. The area of the Cumbrian Mountains is the most rugged in England and is more commonly known as the Lake District because of the many lakes there.

The Pennines, a large chain of hills with moorland tops rising to between 600 and 900 metres, **splits** northern England into northwest and northeast sectors. They run down from the Scottish border to the River Trent about halfway down the country.

The South West is a long peninsula with **bleak** moorlands and rocky outcrop. The wide expanse of Salisbury Plain occupies most of the central part of southern England.

In the South East, a horseshoe-shaped ring of chalk downs surrounds the formerly wooded area of the Weald. The southeast corner, from Dover to Eastbourne, has **dramatic** chalk cliffs bordering the English Channel.

The Longest River in England

England's best known river is, of course, the Thames which flows through London. It is also the longest (346 km) in England. The River Severn is the longest in total, but its source is in the mountains of Wales, and the parts which run through England are shorter than the Thames.

Coastline and the Borders

England has a long coastline of 3,200 km. In the south and west, the coastline can be rocky, with steep cliffs. The east coast is often flat and low lying, with beaches and mud flats.

The English Channel runs along England's southern border, and the North Sea forms England's eastern border. Wales and the Irish Sea border England to the West. Scotland runs along England's northwestern borders.

After You Read

Knowledge Focus

1. Fill in the blanks according to the geographical knowledge you have learned in the text above.
   (1) England is in the _____ part of Great Britain, 35 kilometers from _____. And now they are linked by _____ Tunnel under _____.
   (2) The highest point in England is _____, part of the _____ Mountains in North West England.
   (3) The area in North West England is more commonly known as _____ because of the many lakes there.
   (4) _____, a large chain of hills with moorland tops rising to between 600 and 900 meters, splits northern England into northwest and northeast sectors.
   (5) The longest river in England is _____.
   (6) In the _____ and _____, the coastline of England can be rocky, with steep cliffs. The _____ coast is often flat and low lying, with beaches and mud flats.
   (7) The _____ of England is a long peninsular with bleak moorlands and rocky outcrop.
   (8) _____ and the _____ Sea border England to the West.

2. Write T in the brackets if the statement is true and write F if it is false.
   (1) England is an island country and also part of the United Kingdom. (　)
   (2) England is the smallest country in Great Britain and the UK. (　)
   (3) Much of the land in England is low lying. (　)
   (4) The highest point in England is Scafell Pike, part of the Grampian Mountains in North West England. (　)
   (5) England's best known river is the Thames which flows through London. It is also

the longest in the UK. ( )

(6) England has a long coastline. In the south and west, the coast is often flat and low lying. ( )

(7) The landscape of England is more rugged in the north and the west. ( )

(8) Scotland runs along England's western borders. ( )

Language Focus

1. Fill in the blanks with the proper form of the words or phrases below.

split	confine...to	be known as	in total
underlie	in reference to	offence	comprise

(1) England is sometimes wrongly used _____ the whole United Kingdom, the entire island of Great Britain, or indeed the British Isles.

(2) Upland areas are generally _____ northern England.

(3) The River Severn is the longest _____ in the UK.

(4) The incorrect reference can cause _____ to people from Scotland, Wales and Northern Ireland.

(5) The Pennines _____ northern England into northwest and northeast sectors.

(6) The area of the Cumbrian Mountains is the most rugged in England and is more commonly _____ the Lake District.

(7) Different types of rock _____ the landscape.

(8) Three countries _____ the island of Britain.

2. Fill in the blanks with the appropriate form of the words in the brackets.

(1) It is _____ (correct) to use England in reference to the UK, and it can cause _____ (offensive) to people from other parts of the UK.

(2) The highest _____ (elevate) are in Cumbria and the Lake District in the west.

(3) The landscape of England is _____ (determination) by the different types of rock _____ (underlie) it.

(4) England is the largest of the countries _____ (comprisable) the island of Britain.

(5) Upland areas are generally _____ (confinement) to northern England.

(6) Nearly 84% of the population of the UK lives in England, mainly in the major cities and _____ (metropolis) areas.

(7) In the south and west, the coastline can be _____ (rock), with steep cliffs.

(8) The English Channel runs along England's _____ (south) border, and the North Sea forms England's _____ (east) border.

3. Fill in the blanks with the proper prepositions and adverbs that collocate with the neighboring words.

(1) England is only 35 km _____ France and is now linked _____ a tunnel under the English Channel.

(2) It is sometimes, wrongly, used _____ reference _____ the whole United

Kingdom, the entire island of Great Britain, or indeed the British Isles.

(3) No place in England is more than 75 miles (120 km) _____ the sea.

(4) In the south, chalk has produced the gently rolling hills of the Downs, while hard granite is the basis _____ the mountains of the north and the high moorlands of Dartmoor and Exmoor _____ the southwest.

(5) The Pennines are a large chain of hills _____ moorland tops rising _____ between 600 and 900 meters.

(6) The Pennines run down _____ the Scottish border _____ the river Trent about halfway down the country.

(7) The River Severn's source is _____ the mountains of Wales, and the parts which run _____ England are shorter than the Thames.

(8) The English Channel runs _____ England's southern border.

4. **Read the following sentences and tell if it is OK to change the passive voice into the subjective one. Why or why not?**

(1) England is linked with France by a tunnel under the English Channel.

(2) England is sometimes wrongly used in reference to the whole UK, the entire island of Great Britain, or in deed the British Isles.

(3) England is divided into nine regions.

(4) The landscape is determined mainly by the different types of rock underlying it.

(5) Upland areas are generally confined to northern England.

(6) The area of the Cumbrian Mountains is more commonly known as the Lake District because of many lakes there.

(7) He was found lying on the ground.

(8) They were seen to enter the building.

Comprehensive Work

Solo Work: Suppose you are English, living in England, and write to one of your friends in China, introducing England. You can write a letter, a poem or lyrics.

_____
_____
_____
_____
_____
_____
_____
_____
_____
_____

Read More

Text B   **Climate in England**

Read the passage quickly and figure out the answer to the following questions.
1. Select the probable meaning of the underlined words in the passage.

   (1) predict _____
      A. control   B. talk about   C. tell in advance   D. overwhelm
   (2) temperate _____
      A. warm   B. lower   C. operated   D. mild
   (3) maritime _____
      A. characteristic of the sea   B. chronological
      C. connected with martial   D. maternal
   (4) damp _____
      A. wet   B. sunny   C. dry   D. windy
   (5) subject to _____
      A. addicted to   B. necessary for   C. superior to   D. dependent on
   (6) precipitation _____
      A. moisture   B. wetness   C. the falling of water   D. air pressure
   (7) proximity _____
      A. nearness   B. ownership   C. probability   D. proximal
   (8) mean _____
      A. imply   B. stingy   C. awful   D. average

2. Write T in the brackets if the statement is true and write F if it is false.
   (1) Since the climate in England is mild on the whole, it's easy to tell the weather in the following days. (　)
   (2) The summer and winter in England are cooler than those in the continent. (　)
   (3) In England, July and August are normally the warmest months, and February the coldest. (　)
   (4) To travel in England in July is probably not a good choice since it is the hottest. (　)
   (5) The Warm Current of Mexico Gulf, the Atlantic Ocean and the Southern Latitude all influence the climate in England. (　)
   (6) Compared with other land masses, England is more influenced by the ocean, because it is much closer to the ocean. (　)
   (7) During the months of the longest daylight, the average duration of the sunshine every day can reach 8 hours in some place in England. (　)

Temperature

Britain is an island country and the surrounding sea gives England a varied climate. We never know what the weather will be like from one day to the other. It can be sunny one day and rainy the next. As we have such a variable climate changing from day to day, it is difficult to predict the weather. In general, it has warm summers and cool winters. Its summers are cooler than those on the continent, but the winters are milder.

1. Temperate Climate

The overall climate in England is called temperate maritime. This means that it is mild with temperatures not much lower than 0 ℃ in winter and not much higher than 32 ℃ in summer. It also means that it is damp and is subject to frequent changes.

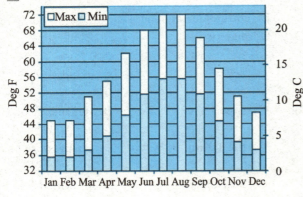

2. Warmest and coldest months

July and August are normally the warmest month in England. Around the coasts, February is normally the coldest month, but inland there is little to choose between January and February as the coldest month.

3. Best months to travel to England

Probably the best months to travel in England are May, June, September and October. These months generally have more pleasant temperatures and less rain. July and August are the warmest months, but they are also the wettest. The sunniest parts of the Britain are along the south coast of England.

June and July, 2007 have been the wettest months England has had for years. Many places have been flooded. August is turning out to be hot and dry.

Rainfall

Rain is fairly well distributed throughout the year, with late winter/spring (February to March) the driest period and autumn/

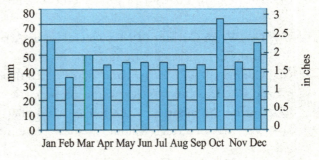

winter (October to January) the wettest.

The Lake District is England's wettest region, receiving an average of 130 inches (330 centimeters) of <u>precipitation</u> each year. The western and northern hills receive about 40 inches (102 centimeters) of rain, while the east coast receives about 20 inches (51 centimeters).

* *Interesting Fact*
Autumn 2000 was the wettest since records began in 1766, with a total of 503 millimeters of rainfall for September, October and November.

What Influences the Weather?

The main influence on the climate is the close <u>proximity</u> to the Atlantic Ocean, the northern latitude, and the warming of the waters around the land by the Gulf Stream (a warm current of the northern Atlantic Ocean).

The island is small compared with the other land masses in the northern hemisphere—hence Britain is more influenced by the ocean compared with other European countries, and the Gulf Stream helps to keep winters milder compared with other landlocked nations with a similar latitude.

Sunshine

During June, July and August (the months of longest daylight), the <u>mean</u> daily duration of sunshine varies from five hours in northern Scotland to eight hours in the Isle of Wight.

During the months of shortest daylight (November, December and January), sunshine is at a minimum, with an average of an hour a day in northern Scotland and two hours a day on the south coast of England.

* *Interesting Fact*
The highest monthly total of sunshine on record is 384 hours in Eastbourne and Hasting, Sussex, in July 1911.

Proper Nouns

Cumbria 坎布里亚郡
Dover 多佛尔
Eastbourne 伊斯特本市(位于东萨塞克斯郡)
Scafell Pike 斯科菲峰
Stonehenge 史前巨石阵(位于威尔特郡)

the Cumbrian Mountains 坎布里亚山脉
the Downs 唐斯丘陵
the Salisbury Plain 索尔兹伯里平原
the Weald 韦尔德地带(在英格兰东南部,旧时为原始密林地带)

Websites to visit

http://en.wikipedia.org/wiki/Flag_of_England

  This is a webpage about the Flag of England, on which you can find such information as history, incorporation into the union, etc.

http://en.wikipedia.org/wiki/Scafell_Pike

  This is a webpage about the Scafell Pike, the highest mountain in England.

Books to read

The Rough Guide to England 8 by Jonathan Buckley et al.

  The guide takes a detailed look at England's history, literature, politics and cultural life with a brand new section on music and expert background on everything from English beer to Thomas Hardy's Wessex. There's plenty of practical advice for experiencing the great outdoors, from cycling coast to coast, to hiking in the Yorkshire Dales; information on all the best accommodation, transportation and restaurants plus lively reviews of hundreds of shops, bars and clubs. Explore every corner of England with the clearest maps of any guide.

England, My England: A Treasury of All Things English by Gerry Hanson

  It is a great discovery—a lovely mix of prose, poetry and information. Gerry Hanson has researched a wide variety of sources—from Shakespeare through to Jeremy Paxman. There is humour, pathos and tears, and the subjects vary from Cricket to Roast Beef.

Movies to see

Elizabeth (1998)

  It is a film of the early years of the reign of Elizabeth I of England and her difficult task of learning what is necessary to be a monarch.

Elizabeth: the Golden Age (2007)

A mature Queen Elizabeth endures multiple crises late in her reign including court intrigues, an assassination plot, the Spanish Armada, and romantic disappointments.

This is England (2006)

It is a story about a troubled boy growing up in England, set in 1983. He comes across a few skinheads on his way home from school, after a fight. They become his new best friends even like family.

Songs to enjoy

There'll Always Be an England
Music by Ross Parker & Harry Parr-Davies
Lyrics by Hugh Charles

I give you a toast, ladies and gentlemen.
I give you a toast, ladies and gentlemen.
May this fair dear land we love so well
In dignity and freedom dwell.
Though worlds may change and go awry
While there is still one voice to cry—
There'll always be an England
While there's a country lane,
Wherever there's a cottage small
Beside a field of grain.
There'll always be an England
While there's a busy street,

Wherever there's a turning wheel,
A million marching feet.
Red, white and blue; what does it mean to you?
Surely you're proud, shout it aloud,
"Britons, awake!"
The empire too, we can depend on you.
Freedom remains. These are the chains
Nothing can break.
There'll always be an England,
And England shall be free
If England means as much to you
As England means to me.

Land of Hope and Glory

Music by Sir Edward Elgar
Words by A.C. Benson

Land of Hope and Glory, Mother of the Free,
How shall we extol thee, who are born of thee?
Wider still, and wider, shall thy bounds be set;
God, who made thee mighty, make thee mightier yet!

Truth and Right and Freedom, each a holy gem,
Stars of solemn brightness, weave thy diadem.

Tho' thy way be darkened, still in splendour drest,
As the star that trembles o'er the liquid West.

Throned amid the billows, throned inviolate,
Thou hast reigned victorious, thou has smiled at fate.

Land of Hope and Glory, fortress of the Free,
How may we extol thee, praise thee, honour thee?

Hark, a mighty nation maketh glad reply;
Lo, our lips are thankful, lo, our hearts are high!

Hearts in hope uplifted, loyal lips that sing;
Strong in faith and freedom, we have crowned our King!

Unit 3
South West England

> Much of what has been written about Stonehenge is derivative, second-rate or plain wrong.
> —Christopher Chippindale

Unit Goals

- To have a general idea of the geography of South West England
- To be familiar with the geographical terms about South West England
- To be able to introduce south West England
- To be able to describe Stonehenge, Bristol and Bath
- To be able to make a comparison between South West and South East
- To be able to use the there-be sentence more skillfully

Before You Read

1. Have you ever heard of the city of Bath located in South West England? Is it a city where you can have a bath? Can you guess its origin?
2. What does the picture on the right show? Where is it? Is it mysterious? What do you think its functions are?
3. What does the picture on the right show? It is something that South West England is famous for!

25

4. South West England is known for producing Cheddar _____, a food consisting of proteins and fat from milk and building strong bones and teeth.
5. **Group Work**: Form groups of three or four students. Try to find, on the Internet or in the library, more information about South West England, for example, its landscape, its economy, or its World Heritage Sites (the city of Bath, the Jurassic Coast, Stonehenge), which interests you most. Get ready for a 5-minute presentation in class.

Start to Read

Text A — View of South West

Location and Composition

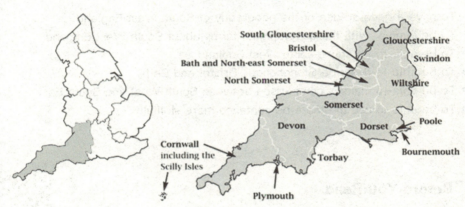

The South West is the largest of the English regions covering the historic counties of Cornwall, Devon, Dorset, Gloucestershire, Somerset and Wiltshire, the unitary authorities of Bath and North East Somerset, Borough of Poole, Bournemouth, Bristol, North Somerset, Plymouth, South Gloucestershire, Swindon and Torbay, together with the Isles of Scilly. The region has **distinctive** sub-regional identities, largely defined by its diverse geography.

Landscape

The South West is a long peninsular with bleak moorlands and rocky outcrop. The region's main rivers are the Severn, Britain's longest river, which **empties into** the Bristol Channel, and the Avon, which flows through the city of Bristol.

The wide expanse of Salisbury Plain occupies most of the central part of southern England. It covers an area of approximately 300 square miles (775 sq km) and is drained to the south by the River Avon. Salisbury plain is a **barren** chalk plateau without trees and much of it is used as a pasture for sheep. Many people travel to see Stonehenge, a **prehistoric** monument located on Salisbury Plain.

The region is one of the most attractive in Europe. It contains significant areas of international and national **designations** for nature **conservation** and landscape, and has large **proportions** of the country's undeveloped coast. The region has two National Parks, Exmoor and Dartmoor, attracting millions of visitors each year and a third of its area is **classified as** part of an Area of Outstanding Natural Beauty (AONB).

There are over 900 Sites of Special Scientific Interest, 638 km of designated Heritage Coast (61% of the total for England) and over 40 National Nature Reserves. It is the most rural, with over half of the population living in rural areas and has the longest stretch of coastline of any English region.

The region also contains important **archaeological** sites including over 6,000 ancient monuments, over 108,000 listed buildings and three World Heritage Sites. These are Stonehenge, Avebury; the City of Bath; and the "Jurassic Coast" of Devon and Dorset that has the **distinction** of being the first natural landscape on the UK mainland to be awarded World Heritage Site status.

Important Cities

Bristol is the region's biggest city, and is also an important port whose fortunes were founded in the 1700s on the slave trade. Slaves were brought here from West Africa. Smaller ports in the region include Weymouth, Poole and Plymouth. Ferry services to continental Europe operate from all these ports. Other important cities and towns include the Roman cities of Bath and Gloucester, and the historic cathedral cities of Exeter and Salisbury.

Specialties and Industry

The South West is known for its draught cider and clotted cream teas.

There are cob-and-thatched cottages, fishing villages and shady creeks. The region covers most of an area known as the West Country, i.e. Devon, Cornwall and Somerset. They are very popular as holiday destinations. Because of this, there are lots of hotels, caravan and camp sites and B & B's, bed and breakfast-houses that offer rooms and breakfasts.

The South West of England is well known for producing Cheddar cheese, named after Cheddar gorge, which is located close to Bristol, and for cider.

Cornwall used to be famous for its tin mines, which operated from Roman times until the last mine closed in 1998.

There are stone and clay quarries in Devon and Cornwall. Other regional industries include engineering, ship building, electronics and food processing. Swindon is home to many new industries, such as computers. Japanese car manufacturer Honda has an important car plant just outside Swindon.

Many individuals and groups in Cornwall maintain that Cornwall is not a part of England and assert that constitutionally it is a Duchy and nation of the UK. Cornwall has a **distinctive** culture, identity and language, separate from the rest of England.

After You Read

Knowledge Focus

1. **Fill in the blanks according to the geographical knowledge you have learned in the text above.**
   (1) The wild granite plateau of _____ in Devon, with its rocky outcrops, dramatic gorges and valleys, is a national park. _____, further north, is a bracken-covered hilly moorland.
   (2) A third of the area in the South West of England is classified as part of an _____ (AONB).
   (3) South West England contains important archaeological sites and three _____. These are _____, Avebury; the city of _____; and the "_____" of Devon and Dorset that has the distinction of being the first natural landscape on the UK mainland to be awarded World Heritage Site status.
   (4) The West Country includes Cornwall, _____, and _____.
   (5) The wide expanse of _____ Plain occupies most of the central part of southern England. It covers an area of approximately 300 square miles (775 sq km) and is drained to the south by _____.
   (6) _____ is the biggest city in South West England; Exeter and _____ are the historic cathedral cities.

2. Write T in the brackets if the statement is true and write F if it is false.
   (1) South West England is the largest of the English regions. （　）
   (2) South West England has two National Parks and an Area of Outstanding Natural Beauty. （　）
   (3) Cornwall, the city of Bath, and the "Jurassic Coast" of Devon are the three World Heritage Sites in South West England. （　）
   (4) The main rivers in South West England are the Severn and the Avon. （　）
   (5) The wide expanse of Salisbury Plain occupies most of the central part of northern England. （　）
   (6) Bristol is the biggest city in South West England, and is also an important port whose fortunes were founded in the 1700s on foreign trade. （　）

Language Focus

1. Fill in the blanks with the proper form of the phrases below.

be separate from	name after	be used as	classify...as
be known for	used to be	empty into	because of

   (1) A third of its area _____ part of an Area of Outstanding Natural Beauty (AONB).
   (2) The South West _____ its draught cider and clotted cream teas.
   (3) They are very popular as holiday destinations. _____ this, there are lots of hotels, caravan and camp sites and B&B's.
   (4) The Severn, Britain's longest river, _____ the Bristol Channel.
   (5) Much of the plain _____ a pasture for sheep.
   (6) The South West of England is well known for producing Cheddar cheese, _____ Cheddar gorge.
   (7) Cornwall _____ be famous for its tin mines, which operated from Roman times until the last mine closed in 1998.
   (8) Cornwall has a distinctive culture, identity and language, _____ the rest of England.

2. Fill in the blanks with the appropriate form of the words in the brackets.
   (1) The region has _____ (distinction) sub-regional _____ (identify), largely defined by its diverse geography.
   (2) South West England contains significant areas of international and national designations for nature _____ (conserve) and landscape, and has large _____ (proportionate) of the country's undeveloped coast.
   (3) The region also contains important _____ (archeology) sites.
   (4) There are over 900 Sites of Special _____ (Science) Interest, 638 km of _____ (designation) Heritage Coast (61% of the total for England) and over 40 National Nature Reserves.
   (5) There are cob-and-thatched cottages, fishing villages and _____ (shade) creeks.
   (6) Many people travel to see Stonehenge, a _____ (history) monument, _____

(locate) on Salisbury Plain.

(7) There are stone and clay quarries in Devon and Cornwall. Other regional industries include _____ (engineer), ship building, _____ (electronic) and food _____ (process).

(8) Many individuals and groups in Cornwall _____ (maintenance) that Cornwall is not a part of England and assert that _____ (constitution) it is a Duchy and nation of the UK.

3. Fill in the blanks with the proper prepositions and adverbs that collocate with the neighboring words.

(1) The region has distinctive sub-regional identities, largely defined _____ its diverse geography.

(2) The South West contains significant areas of international and national designations _____ nature conservation and landscape.

(3) Dorset that has the distinction _____ being the first natural landscape _____ the UK mainland to be awarded World Heritage Site status.

(4) The region covers most of an area known _____ the West Country, i.e. Devon, Cornwall and Somerset.

(5) The Avon flows _____ the city of Bristol.

(6) It covers an area of approximately 300 square miles and is drained _____ the south by the River Avon.

(7) Salisbury plain is a barren chalk plateau _____ trees.

(8) Slaves were brought into Bristol _____ West Africa.

4. Fill in the blanks in the following there-be sentences.

(1) There _____ over 900 sites of Special Scientific Interest, 638 km of designated Heritage Coast and over 400 National Nature Reserves.

(2) There _____ cob-and-thatched cottages, fishing villages and shady creeks.

(3) There _____ stone and clay quarries in Devon and Cornwall.

(4) There seems something wrong about it, _____ it?

(5) There _____ no buses, we had to go home on foot.

(6) There _____ great changes in our school since last year.

(7) I hear that it is fairly common in Africa for there _____ a group of expert musicians surrounded by others who also join in the performances.

(8) The waiter spilled wine on the carpet, but there _____ no harm done.

Comprehensive Work

1. Pair Work: Discuss the cartoon below with your partner.

(1) Where are they?

(2) Who are they, historians, archaeologists, or tourists? And where are they from?

(3) What are they talking about? What do they mean?

"Maybe it has something to do with 'Feng Shui'."

2. **Solo Work:** Fill in the blanks in the following graph with the information you have acquired in the text. And then share yours with your partner.

South West England				
National Parks	World Heritage	Major Rivers	Industries	Regional Specialties

3. **Solo Work:** Use your imagination and make a wild guess of why Stonehenge was built. Make it as interesting as possible. Write down your imagined story within 300 words and share it with your classmates.

Read More

Text B   The Origin of Bath

Read the passage quickly and select the probable meaning of the underlined words in the passage.

1. succeed _____
    A. completely defeat   B. do what one has tried or wanted to do
    C. live up to   D. be the next to take a position or rank

2. dedicated _____
   A. devoted
   B. decorated
   C. designated
   D. definitive
3. inextinguishable _____
   A. very large
   B. not able to distinguish
   C. impossible to put an end to
   D. stingy
4. disguise _____
   A. a difficult situation
   B. one's dream
   C. sth. to hide who one really is
   D. great anger
5. swineherd _____
   A. a person to protect Swainswick
   B. a herd of pigs
   C. a person to make wine
   D. a laundry worker
6. wallow _____
   A. roll around
   B. swallow
   C. get sick
   D. be scared
7. mire _____
   A. embarrassment
   B. mud
   C. water
   D. fire
8. inheritance _____
   A. health
   B. circumstance
   C. title or property inherited
   D. motherland

Bladud, the British King who learnt to fly, is one of the most remarkable characters to figure in Bath's history. Even if there is no truth in the Bladud myth, it still provides us with a fascinating story about the origins of Bath.

Bladud became the ninth King of the Britons in 863 B.C. succeeding his father Ludhudibras. Educated at Athens, he returned on his father's death accompanied by four philosophers. He founded a university at Stamford in Lincolnshire, and by practicing necromancy he created the hot springs at Bath. Here he founded a temple dedicated to Minerva and placed the inextinguishable fires. He made feathered wings and learnt to fly but fell on the Temple of Apollo at New Troy and broke his neck, after reigning 20 years. He was succeeded by his son King Lear.

Bladud spent eleven years at Athens and returned home a leper. Because of his illness he was confined but escaped in disguise from his father's court and came to a place called Swainswick where he was employed as a swineherd. In cold weather he saw his pigs wallowing in a mire. He found that the mud was warm and the pigs enjoyed the heat. Noticing that the pigs which bathed in the mire were free of scurf and scabs, and reasoning that he might benefit in the same way, he too bathed in the waters and was duly cured of leprosy. He revealed his identity to his master and returned to has father's court where he was recognized and restored to his <u>inheritance</u>. He succeeded to the throne on his father's death, whereupon he founded the City of Bath around the hot springs and built the baths so that others might benefit as he had done.

Text C Stonehenge

Read the passage quickly and try to find the information to fill in the blanks below.

_____ said Stonehenge may have been an ancient _____ site for the sick, because the bluestones with _____ qualities were revered as _____ stones and a number of the _____ around Stonehenge showed signs of trauma and deformity. During the research, they also found that Stonehenge was not just a _____ monument; it was a _____ and _____ monument.

In this Monday March 31, 2008 file photo, archaeology students Steve Bush, right, and Sam Ferguson, left, <u>sieved</u> through earth amongst the stones at Stonehenge, England.

Archaeologists probing the secrets of Stonehenge, Britain's most famous prehistoric monument, said on Monday it may have been an ancient pilgrimage site for the sick who believed its stones had healing qualities.

It has always been a mystery why bluestones, the smaller stones that form part of the circle, were transported around 155 miles from Preseli Hills in Wales to Wiltshire in southern England.

Archaeologists from Bournemouth University, who carried out the dig in April—the first at Stonehenge since 1964—believed the bluestones were <u>revered</u> as healing stones.

"It was the magical qualities of these stones which... transformed the monument and made it a place of pilgrimage for the sick and injured of the Neolithic world," a statement from the archaeologist team said.

Geoffrey Wainwright, president of the Society of Antiquaries of London and one of the experts leading the work, told BBC radio that one reason which led to the conclusion was that a number of the burials around Stonehenge showed signs of **trauma** and **deformity**.

The archaeologists said in the statement that radio-carbon dating put the construction of the circle of bluestones at between 2,400 B.C. and 2,200 B.C., a few centuries later than originally thought.

But they found fragments of charcoal dating from before 7,000 B.C., showing humans were active in the area much earlier than previously thought.

During the **excavation** at the World Heritage Site on Salisbury Plain, the researchers also found a beaker pottery fragment, Roman ceramics and ancient stone hammers.

"We now know, much to our surprise and delight, that Stonehenge was not just a prehistoric monument; it was a Roman and mediaeval monument," said Wainwright.

Another of the team leaders, Tim Darvill of Bournemouth University, said the bluestones appeared central to the purpose of Stonehenge although it may have had more than one function.

Other theories about Stonehenge are that it was a religious site or that it acted as a calendar.

Proper Nouns

Avebury 埃夫伯里巨石圈
AONB（英）杰出自然风景区
Bath 巴斯城
Bath and North East Somerset 巴斯及东北萨摩赛特郡
Bladud （传说中的）布拉杜德国王
Borough of Poole 普尔市
Bournemouth 伯恩茅斯市
Bristol 布里斯托尔市
Cornwall 康沃尔郡
Exeter 埃克塞特市
Gloucester 格洛斯特市
Gloucestershire 格洛斯特郡

Minerva 罗马神话中的智慧女神密涅瓦
North Somerset 北萨摩赛特郡
Plymouth 普利茅斯市
Salisbury 索尔兹伯里市
South Gloucestershire 南格洛斯特郡
Swainswick 斯万维克
Swindon 斯文登
the Bristol Channel 布里斯托尔海峡
the "Jurassic Coast" 侏罗纪海岸
the Society of Antiquaries （伦敦）古文物学会
Torbay 托培
Weymouth 威矛斯市
Wiltshire 威尔特郡

For Fun

Websites to visit
http://en.wikipedia.org/wiki/South_West_England

This is a webpage about South West England, on which you can read information on its geography, history, industry, economy, etc.

http://whc.unesco.org/en/list/373

This is a webpage about Stonehenge, Avebury and Associated Sites.

http://www.bathnes.gov.uk/future/Bath/Identity+and+Vision/The+soul+of+Bath.htm

This is a webpage about Bath's soul, on which you can find such information as its hot springs, its social and cultural renaissance, its growth of industry, etc.

http://www.kingbladudspigs.org/

This is a website on which you can read all kinds of information on King Bladud's Pigs in Bath.

Books to read

The Return of the Native by Thomas Hardy

Set in Egdon Heath, a wild tract of country in the southwest of England, this is a masterpiece of dramatic tension. Clym Yeobright, a diamond merchant in Paris, returns to his home in Egdon where he falls passionately in love with the sensuous, free-spirited Eustacia Vye. She, while in a brief state of infatuation, marries him, hoping he will take her away to the more exciting life in Paris. But Eustacia's dreams of escape are not to be realized. Clym Yeobright, the returning native, can not bring her salvation.

In *The Return of the Native* there is a strong conflict between nature or fate, represented by Egdon Heath, and human nature, represented by Hardy's true-to-life characters. This is a novel which perfectly epitomizes Thomas Hardy's unique and melancholy genius.

Far from the Madding Crowd by Thomas Hardy

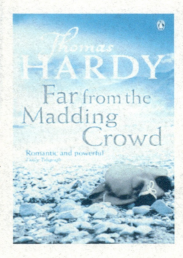

"I shall do one thing in this life—one thing for certain—that is, love you, and long for you, and keep wanting you till I die." Gabriel Oak is only one of three suitors for the hand of the beautiful and spirited Bathsheba Everdene. He must compete with the dashing young soldier Sergeant Troy and respectable, middle-aged Farmer Boldwood. And while their fates depend upon the choice Bathsheba makes, she discovers the terrible consequences of an inconstant heart. *Far From the Madding Crowd* was the first of Hardy's novels to give the name of Wessex to the landscape of south-west England, and the first to gain him widespread popularity as a novelist. Set against the backdrop of the unchanging natural cycle of the year, the story both upholds and questions rural values with a startlingly modern sensibility. This new edition retains the critical text that restores previously deleted and revised passages.

Movies to see

Hot Fuzz（2007）

Jealous colleagues conspire to get a top London cop transferred to the sleepy and seemingly crime-free village of Sandford in rural Gloucestershire and paired with a witless new partner. On the beat, the pair stumble upon a series of suspicious accidents and events.

Northanger Abbey（BBC 1986）

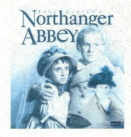

Jane Austen's novel *Northanger Abbey* (1818) was adapted for television in 1986 by the A&E Network and the BBC. Catherine Morland is a young woman who enjoys reading Gothic Novels. She is invited to Bath by a family friend, Mrs. Allen, and there she meets Henry Tilney and his sister Eleanor. Upon returning to her home with her family Eleanor invites Catherine to come along as her guest and companion. There Catherine's imagination continues to flourish and she starts to suspect a dark secret at Northanger Abbey.

Music to enjoy

A Morning in Cornwall
by James Last

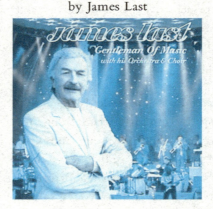

Unit 4
South East England

> So poetry, which is in Oxford made / An art, in London only is a trade.
>
> — John Dryden

Unit Goals

- To have a general idea of the geography of South East England
- To be familiar with the geographical terms about South East England
- To be able to introduce South East England
- To be able to describe the chalk cliffs, Oxford and Canterbury
- To be able to watch the subject-verb agreement in sentences

Before You Read

1. _____ is the largest city in South East England. It is nicknamed *The City of* _____ *Spires*. It is famous worldwide for its _____, the oldest university in the English-speaking world.

2. Do you know the spiritual capital of England? It is _____ in _____ in South East England. It is one of the most important pilgrimage destinations in Europe. _____'s famous *The Canterbury Tales*, written in the 14th century, is about a mix of pilgrims telling each other stories to pass the time on their pilgrimage from _____ to _____.

3. _____ is situated in Kent, on England's southeastern tip and is the UK's closest geographical point to Continental _____.

4. _____, known as the "Garden of England", is famous for its apples and for hops, used in brewing beer.
5. **Group Work:** Form groups of three or four students. Try to find, on the Internet or in the library, more information about South East England, for example, its landscape, its economy, or its cities, which interests you most. Get ready for a 5-minute presentation in class.

Start to Read

Text A　　View of South East England

Location and Composition

South East England is one of the nine official regions of England. Its boundaries include Berkshire, Buckinghamshire, East Sussex, Hampshire, Isle of Wight, Kent, Oxfordshire, Surrey and West Sussex. The South East is more **densely** populated than any other part of England.

Landscape

South East England is a **mixture** of lowlands and chains of small hills. To the far northwest are the Cotswold Hills, while the Chilterns **extend** from Oxfordshire across Buckinghamshire into Hertfordshire.

The New Forest National Park location is on the south-central coast of England and lies within the county of Hampshire.

A horseshoe-shaped ring of chalk hills known as the Downs runs down to the sea through Kent and Sussex. The South Downs reach the coast near Brighton, the North Downs at Dover, where they end in the famous white cliffs, which are the first sight of England for travelers by sea from continental Europe.

Important Towns and Cities

The M25, the motorway which rings London, is linked by other motorways with the Channel ports of Dover, Southampton and Portsmouth. Dover is England's busiest port. Ferries carry passengers and freight to and from the continent of Europe. The terminus for the Channel Tunnel, which opened in 1994 and links English mainland with the rest of Europe, is at Folkestone.

There are several busy seaside resorts in the South East, including Margate, Worthing, Brighton and Eastbourne. The cathedral cities of Canterbury and Winchester also attract many visitors each year. Other important towns include Reading and Windsor in Berkshire.

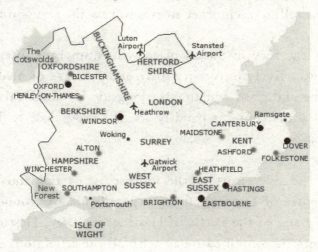

1. Oxford

Oxford, the City of Dreaming Spires, is the first city from the source on the River Thames. It is also the largest city in South East England. It is famous **worldwide** for its University, the oldest university in the English-speaking world. For over 800 years, Oxford has been a home to **royalty**. The first known settlement here grew up in the 8th century around a priory close to a crossing point in the Thames. The settlement was then known as "Oxenaforda".

Oxford's name comes from the crossing point of ford across the Thames. The ford was used by cattle farmers to drive their oxen to market. It is the combination of the words "oxen" and "ford" that gives Oxford its name. (Fords are places where the water is shallow enough to walk across to the opposite bank.)

2. Canterbury

Canterbury is a relatively small city with a population of 45,000, but it is the **spiritual** capital of England.

This was the headquarters and burial place of St. Augustine, the first Archbishop of Canterbury. Augustine was sent from Rome by Pope Gregory to **convert** the English from paganism in 597 A.D. and is **credited with** establishing Christianity in England. Today's Archbishop of Canterbury is the head of the worldwide Anglican Communion.

Canterbury was also the site of the murder of St. Thomas Becket (another Archbishop of Canterbury) in 1170, **at the hands of** the king's knights. Miracles were reported around Thomas' tomb almost immediately and it soon became one of the most important pilgrimage destinations in Europe. Geoffrey Chaucer's famous *The Canterbury Tales*, written in the 14th century, is about a mix of pilgrims telling each other stories to pass the time on their pilgrimage from London.

Canterbury is a very historical place with numerous interesting religious sites. But it is also a lively university town and its maze of medieval streets has excellent shopping and great restaurants alongside its medieval buildings. And **to top it all off**, Canterbury is handily located very close to London and the Eurostar train station.

3. Hastings

Hastings is a seaside resort on the south coast of England, 90 minutes by train from the centre of London. It has a population of around 80,000 and is best known as the site of the Battle of Hastings in 1066. Hastings' importance as a historical centre is combined today with all the attractions and **amenities** of a modern resort, which annually attracts over two million visitors.

4. Dover

Backed by its famous White Cliffs, Dover is situated in Kent, on England's south-eastern tip and is the UK's closest geographical point to Continental Europe. Every day of the year, regular cross Channel ferries travel between the port, Calais and Dunkirk in France, and Ostend in Belgium.

Industry and Farming

The South East has mainly light industries and is also home to the largest oil refinery at Fawley, near Southampton. There are hovercraft factories on the Isle of Wight. Kent has paper mills, shipyards, and a nuclear power station at Dungeness. Away from the towns, there are hundreds of small farms, with orchards and fruit farms. Kent, known as the "Garden of England", is famous for its apples and for hops, used in brewing beer. Lamberhurst is known for its **vineyards** and produces English wines.

Industry in Berkshire centres around Bracknell, Maidenhead, Reading and Slough, with electronics concentrated in Milton Keynes. Hertforshire is known for engineering, mostly at St Albans, Hatfield, Letchworth and Watford. The Oxford suburb of Cowley has huge car factories and was the birthplace of the classic Morris Minor.

After You Read

Knowledge Focus

1. **Fill in the blanks according to the geographical knowledge you have learned in the text above.**
    (1) _____ is the most densely populated region in England.
    (2) South East England is a mixture of _____ and chains of small hills.
    (3) _____ extends from Oxfordshire across Buckinghamshire into Hertfordshire.
    (4) The largest city in South East England is _____.
    (5) _____ was the headquarters and burial place of St Augustine.
    (6) Geoffrey Chaucer's famous _____, written in the 14th century, is about a mix of pilgrims telling each other stories to pass the time on their pilgrimage from London.
    (7) The city of _____ in Kent is the UK's closest geographical point to Continental Europe.
    (8) _____, a seaside resort on the south coast of England, is best known as the site of the Battle in 1066.

2. **Write T in the brackets if the statement is true and write F if it is false.**
    (1) South East England is one of the eight official regions of England. ( )
    (2) The South East is more densely populated than any other part of England. ( )
    (3) South East England is a mixture of lowlands and chains of high mountains. ( )
    (4) Canterbury is a very historical place with numerous interesting religious sites. It does not have excellent shopping and great restaurants alongside its medieval buildings. ( )
    (5) Hastings, a seaside resort on the south coast of England, is best known as the site of the Battle of Hastings in 1966. ( )
    (6) Canterbury is a small city and it is close to London. ( )
    (7) The combination of the words "oxen" and "ford" gives Oxford its name. ( )

Language Focus

1. Fill in the blanks with the proper form of the words or phrases below.

| grow up | worldwide | convert...to | be the birthplace of |
| at the hands of | to top it all off | end in | be credited with |

(1) The South Downs reach the coast near Brighton, the North Downs at Dover, where they _____ the famous white cliffs, which are the first sight of England for travelers by sea from continental Europe.

(2) The first known settlement in Oxford _____ in the 8th century around a priory close to a crossing point in the Thames.

(3) Augustine was sent from Rome by Pope Gregory to _____ the English from paganism _____ Christianity in 597 A.D.

(4) Augustine _____ establishing Christianity in England.

(5) Canterbury was also the site of the murder of St Thomas Becket in 1170, _____ the king's knights.

(6) Oxford is famous _____ for its University, the oldest university in the English-speaking world.

(7) Canterbury is also a lively university town and its maze of medieval streets has excellent shopping and great restaurants alongside its medieval buildings. And, _____ it is handily located very close to London and the Eurostar train station.

(8) The Oxford suburb of Cowley has huge car factories and _____ the classic Morris Minor.

2. Fill in the blanks with the appropriate form of the words in the brackets.

(1) The South East is more densely _____ (population) than any other part of England.

(2) Oxford is famous worldwide for its University, the oldest university in the _____ (speak English) world.

(3) For over 800 years, Oxford has been a home to _____ (royal).

(4) The first known settlement in Oxford grew up in the 8th century around a _____ (prior) close to a crossing point in the Thames.

(5) It is the _____ (combine) of the words "oxen" and "ford" that give Oxford its name.

(6) Canterbury is the _____ (spirit) capital of England.

(7) Augustine was sent by Pope Gregory to _____ (conversion) the English from paganism in 597 A.D.

3. Fill in the blanks with the proper prepositions and adverbs that collocate with the neighboring words.

(1) A horseshoe-shaped ring of chalk hills known _____ the Downs runs down to the sea through Kent and Sussex.

(2) The M25, the motorway which rings London, is linked _____ other motorways _____ the Channel ports of Dover, Southampton and Portsmouth.

(3) Ferries carry passengers and freight _____ and _____ the continent of Europe.
(4) The terminus _____ the Channel Tunnel, which opened in 1994 and links English mainland with the rest of Europe, is _____ Folkestone.
(5) For over 800 years, Oxford has been a home _____ royalty.
(6) Fords are places where the water is shallow enough to walk _____ to the opposite bank.
(7) Today's Archbishop of Canterbury is the head _____ the worldwide Anglican Communion.
(8) Miracles were reported _____ Thomas' tomb almost immediately.

4. **Examine the subject-verb-agreement problems in the following sentences.**
   (1) A horseshoe-shaped ring of chalk hills known as the Downs run down to the sea.
   (2) The South Downs reaches the coast near Brighton, the North Downs at Dover.
   (3) The terminus for the Channel Tunnel, which opened in 1994 and link English mainland with the rest of Europe, are at Folkestone.
   (4) It is the combination of the words "oxen" and "ford" that give Oxford its name.
   (5) Geoffrey Chaucer's famous *The Canterbury Tales*, written in the 14th century, are about a mix of pilgrims telling each other stories to pass the time on their pilgrimage from London.
   (6) My family are not large, but my family is all music lovers.
   (7) He was very angry, because everyone except him were invited to the party.
   (8) He, not you, were criticized by the teacher. In fact, not he but you has been disturbing the other students.

Comprehensive Work

1. **Group Work:** Discuss, in groups of three or four students, the similarities and differences between the landscape in *South West England* and that in *South East England*.

Comparison of Landscape

Items	South West England	South East England
Similarities		
Differences		

2. **Pair Work**: Discuss the following cartoon with your partner.
   (1) What are they doing?
   (2) Who are they respectively?
   (3) What is the humorous point?

"Not a bad term paper, except that I don't think Chaucer ever wrote 'Ye Traveling Salesman's Tale.'"

3. **Solo Work**: Suppose you are an overseas student at the University of Oxford in the South East of England. Write a letter of about 300 words to one of your former classmates in China, persuading him/her to visit Oxford and the surrounding area.

Read More

Text B   Oxford University

Read the passage quickly and finish the following exercises.

1. **Write T in the brackets if the statement is true and write F if it is false.**
   (1) Oxford University is the biggest and oldest university in Britain. ( )
   (2) Oxford University is founded in 12th century as a university for the poor. ( )
   (3) All the colleges in Oxford University take both men and women equally. ( )
   (4) Some Prime Ministers of the UK once studied in Oxford University. ( )

2. **Select the probable meaning of the underlined words in the passage.**
   (1) intellectual _____
       A. emotional   B. rational   C. teller's   D. telecommunication
   (2) prestigious _____
       A. religious   B. present   C. respected   D. ancient
   (3) comparatively _____
       A. not really   B. increasingly   C. coincidentally   D. relatively

There are about ninety universities in Great Britain, and the number has been growing. The biggest one is London University, but the oldest one is Oxford.

Oxford University has been for centuries at Britain's <u>intellectual</u> heart, maybe the most <u>prestigious</u> among Europe's many ancient universities. Oxford was founded in the 12th century as an aristocratic University and maintains its aristocratic character till now. The tuition is comparatively high. Students have to pay for using libraries and laboratories, as well as for taking examinations. It is a collection of 35 colleges: two for women only, the rest taking both men and women. The largest college has over five hundred students; while the smallest college has only one hundred students.

There are many famous politicians who once studied here. They are the 19th-century statesman and four times British Prime Minister William Gladstone, 20th-century Prime Minister Edward Heath and Margaret Thatcher and so on.

Text C   On *The Canterbury Tales*

Read the passage and try to find the answers to the following questions.
1. What is the greatness of Chaucer?
2. What is the content of *The Canterbury Tales*?

Geoffrey Chaucer began writing *The Canterbury Tales* sometime around 1387 A.D.; the uncompleted manuscript was published in 1400, the year he died. Having recently passed the six hundredth anniversary of its publication, the book is still of interest to modern students for several reasons. *The Canterbury Tales* is recognized as the first book of poetry written in the English language. Before Chaucer's time, even poets who lived in England wrote in Italian or Latin, which meant that poetry was only understandable to people of the wealthy, educated class. English was considered low class and **vulgar**. To a great degree, *The Canterbury Tales* helped make it a **legitimate** language to work in. Because of this work, all of the great writers who followed, from Shakespeare to Dryden to Keats to Eliot, owe him a debt of **gratitude**. It is because Chaucer's writing is a written record of the roots from which the modern language grew. Contemporary readers might find his words nearly as difficult to follow as a foreign language, but scholars are **thankful** for the chance to compare Middle English to the language as it is spoken now, to examine its growth.

In the same way that *The Canterbury Tales* gives modern readers a sense of the language at the time, the book also gives a rich, **intricate tapestry** of medieval social life, combining elements of all classes, from nobles to workers, from priests and nuns to drunkards and thieves. The General Prologue alone provides a panoramic view of society that is not like any found elsewhere in all of literature. Students who are not particularly interested in medieval England can appreciate the author's technique in **capturing** the variations of human **temperament** and behavior. Collections of stories were common in Chaucer's time, and some still exist today, but the genius of *The Canterbury Tales* is that the individual stories are presented in a continuing narrative, showing how all of the various pieces of life connect to one another.

It is the story of a group of thirty people who travel as pilgrims to Canterbury (England). The pilgrims, who come from all layers of society, tell stories to each other to kill time while they travel to Canterbury.

If we trust the General Prologue, Chaucer intended that each pilgrim should tell two tales on the way to Canterbury and two tales on the way back. He never finished his enormous project and even the completed tales were not finally **revised**. Scholars are uncertain about the order of the tales. As the printing press had yet to be invented when Chaucer wrote his works, *The Canterbury Tales* has been passed down in several handwritten manuscripts.

Proper Nouns

Berkshire 伯克郡
Bracknell 布拉克内尔
Brighton 布莱顿
Buckinghamshire 白金汉郡
Calais 加莱(法国)
Canterbury 坎特伯雷
Cowley 考雷
Dungeness 邓杰内斯
Dunkirk 敦刻尔克(法国)
Eastbourne 伊斯特本
East Sussex 东萨塞克斯郡
Edward Heath 爱德华·希思
Eurostar 欧洲之星(穿越英吉利海峡的高速豪华列车)
Fawley 福利
Folkestone 福克斯通
Geoffrey Chaucer 杰弗里·乔叟
Hampshire 汉普郡
Hastings 黑斯廷斯
Hatfield 哈特菲尔德
John Dryden 约翰·德莱顿(英国第一位桂冠诗人)
John Keats 约翰·济慈(英国19世纪浪漫主义重要诗人)
Lamberhurst 兰伯赫斯特
Letchworth 莱奇沃斯
Maidenhead 梅登海德
Margaret Thatcher 玛格丽特·萨切尔

Margate 马加特
Milton Keynes 米尔顿·凯恩斯
Morris Minor 小莫里斯(紧凑小轿车)
Ostend 奥斯坦德(比利时)
Oxford 牛津
Oxfordshire 牛津郡
Pope Gregory 罗马教皇格列高利
Portsmouth 朴次茅斯
Reading 雷丁
Slough 斯劳
Southampton 南安普敦
St. Albans 圣奥尔班斯
St. Augustine 圣奥古斯丁(公元597年成为坎特伯雷大主教)
St. Thomas Becket 圣托马斯·贝克特(12世纪坎特伯雷大主教)
Stephen Hawking 史蒂芬·霍金
Surrey 萨里郡
the Anglican Communion 英国圣公会
the Chilterns 奇特恩斯山
the City of Dreaming Spires 梦幻尖塔之城(牛津昵称)
the Cotswold Hills 科次沃尔德丘陵地带
the Downs 唐斯丘陵
the M25 (Motorway) M25高速公路
the New Forest National Park 新森林国家公园
the Royal Society 伦敦皇家学会

T. S. Eliot 艾略特(现代诗歌之父)
Watford 沃特福德
West Sussex 西萨塞克斯郡
William Gladstone 威廉·格莱斯顿
Winchester 温彻斯特
Windsor 温莎
Worthing 沃辛

For Fun

Websites to visit

http://en.wikipedia.org/wiki/South_East_England

  This is a webpage about South East England, on which you can read such information as its historical boundaries, its transport, its economy, its education, etc.

http://www.visitsoutheastengland.com/

  This is a website about South East England, on which you can read all kinds of information on this region, including things to do, where to eat, accommodation, special offers, etc.

Books to read

Jude the Obscure by Thomas Hardy

  Hardy's last work of fiction, *Jude the Obscure* is one of his most gloomily fatalistic, depicting the lives of individuals who are trapped by forces beyond their control. Jude Fawley, a poor villager, wants to enter the divinity school at Christminster (Oxford University). Sidetracked by Arabella Donn, an earthy country girl who pretends to be pregnant by him, Jude marries her and is then deserted. He earns a living as a stonemason at Christminster; there he falls in love with his independent-minded cousin, Sue Bridehead. Out of a sense of obligation, Sue marries the schoolmaster Phillotson, who has helped her. Unable to bear living with Phillotson, she returns to live with Jude and eventually bears his children out of wedlock. Their poverty and the weight of society's disapproval begin to take a toll on Sue and Jude; the climax occurs when Jude's son by Arabella hangs Sue and Jude's children and himself. In penance, Sue returns to Phillotson and the church. Jude returns to Arabella and eventually dies miserably. The novel's sexual frankness shocked the public, as did Hardy's criticisms of marriage, the university system, and the church. Hardy was so distressed by its reception that he wrote no more fiction, concentrating solely on his poetry.

The Canterbury Tales by Geoffrey Chaucer

  It is a collection of stories written by Geoffrey Chaucer in the 14th century (two of them in prose, the rest in verse). The tales, some of which are originals and others not, are contained inside a frame tale and told by a collection of pilgrims on a pilgrimage from

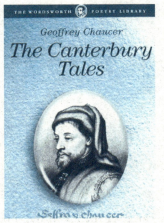
London Borough of Southwark to visit the shrine of Saint Thomas Becket at Canterbury Cathedral. *The Canterbury Tales* are written in Middle English. Although the tales are considered to be his magnum opus, some believe the structure of the tales is indebted to the works of *The Decameron*, which Chaucer is said to have read on an earlier visit to Italy.

Movies to see

Last Orders (2001)

Jack Dodd was a London butcher who enjoyed a pint with his mates for over 50 years. When he died, he died as he lived, with a smile on his face watching a horse race on which he had bet, with borrowed money. But before he died he had a final request, "Last Orders", that his ashes be scattered in the sea at Margate. The movie follows his mates, Ray, Lenny and Vic and his foster son Vince as they journey to the sea with the ashes. Along the way, the threads of their lives, their loves and their disappointments are woven together in their memories of Jack and his wife Amy.

The Oxford Murders (2008)

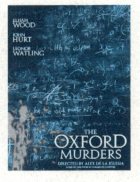

It is a 2008 thriller film adapted from an award-winning novel of the same name by the Argentine mathematician and writer Guillermo Martínez.

At Oxford University, a professor and a grad student work together to try to stop a potential series of murders seemingly linked by mathematical symbols.

The Canterbury Tales (TV Series 2003)

It is a dramatic anthology series that aired on BBC One. Each episode is an adaptation of one of Geoffrey Chaucer's 14th century Canterbury Tales which are transferred to a modern setting. The series first aired in September 2003 and ended after six episodes on October 16, 2003.

Song to enjoy

White Cliffs of Dover (1942)
Lyrics by Nat Burton
Melody by Walter Kent

There'll be bluebirds over the white cliffs of Dover
Tomorrow, just you wait and see
There'll be love and laughter and peace ever after
Tomorrow when the world is free
(The shepherd will tend his sheep)
(The valley will bloom again)

And Jimmy will go to sleep
In his own little room again
There'll be bluebirds over the white cliffs of Dover
Tomorrow, just you wait and see
There'll be bluebirds over the white cliffs of Dover
Tomorrow, just you wait...and see

Unit 5
London

> You find no man, at all intellectual, who is willing to leave London. No, Sir, when a man is tired of London, he is tired of life; for there is in London all that life can afford.
> — Samuel Johnson

Unit Goals

- To have a general idea of the geography of London
- To be familiar with the geographical terms about London
- To be able to tell differences among Greater London, London and the City of London
- To be able to introduce the landmarks in London
- To be able to compare and contrast London and Beijing
- To be able to use the verb tenses properly

Before You Read

1. _____ is the biggest city in Britain. Does "London" equal "the City of London"?

2. London was the first city in the world to have an underground railway, known as the _____.

3. Some of the most important people from countries all over the world visit the Queen at _____ in London, where a familiar sight is _____ ceremony.

UNDERGROUND

4. For over 900 years, _____ has been one of the capital's most prominent landmarks and a world-famous visitor attraction. Throughout its long history, it has served as a royal palace and fortress, prison and place of execution, an arsenal, royal mint, menagerie and jewel house.

5. **Group Work**: Form groups of three or four students. Try to find, on the Internet or in the library, more information about London, for example, its landscape, its economy, its culture or its landmarks, which interests you. Get ready for a 5-minute presentation in class.

Start to Read

| Text A | Greater London and the City of London |

View of Greater London

Greater London is the top-level administrative subdivision covering London, England. The administrative area was created in 1965 and covers the City of London and 32 London boroughs. The Greater London region has by far the highest GDP per capita in the United Kingdom.

It covers 1579 km² (609 square miles) and had a 2006 mid-year estimated population of 7,512,400. It is bounded by the Home Counties of Essex and Hertfordshire in the East of England region and Buckinghamshire, Berkshire, Surrey and Kent in South East England. The highest point in London is Westerham Heights, in the North Downs and on the boundary with Kent, at 245 meters (804 feet).

Greater London is the 37th largest urban area in the world. Its primary geographical feature is the Thames, a **navigable** river which crosses the city from the southwest to the east. The Thames Valley is a floodplain surrounded by gently rolling hills such as Parliament Hill, Addington Hills, and Primrose Hill. These hills **presented** no significant obstacle to the growth of London from its origins as a port on the north side of the river, and therefore London is roughly circular. Many of the highest points in London are located in the suburbs or on the boundaries with adjacent counties.

The Thames was once a much broader, shallower river with extensive marshlands; at high tide, its shores reached five times their current width. Since the Victorian era it has been extensively embanked, and many of its London tributaries now flow underground. The Thames is a tidal river, and London is vulnerable to flooding. The threat has increased over time due to a slow but continuous rise in high water level by the slow "tilting" of Britain (up in the north and down in the south) caused by post-glacial rebound. In 1974, a decade of work began on the construction of the Thames Barrier across the Thames at Woolwich to deal with this threat. While the barrier is expected to function as designed until roughly 2030, concepts for its future enlargement or redesign are already being discussed.

View of the City of London

The City of London is a geographically small city within Greater London, England. It is the historic core of London around which, along with Westminster, the modern conurbation grew. The City's boundaries have remained almost constant since the Middle Ages, and hence it is now only a tiny part of the much larger London metropolis. It is often referred to as just the City or as the Square Mile, as it is almost exactly one square mile (2.6 km^2) in area.

These terms are also often used as metonyms for the United Kingdom's financial services industry, which is principally based there. It should be noted that the City is not one of the 32 London boroughs.

In the medieval period, the City was the full extent of London, and distinct from the nearby. The term London now refers to a much larger conurbation containing both "cities". The City of London is still part of London's city centre, but apart from financial services, most of London's metropolitan functions are centered on the West End. The City is today a major business and financial centre, ranking on a par with New York City as the leading centre of global finance. The City has a resident population of under 10,000, whilst the City employs 340,000 professional workers, mainly in the financial sector, who commute on a daily basis—making the area's transport system extremely busy during certain peak times.

The City is governed by the City of London Corporation, which has some unusual responsibilities for a local authority, such as being the police authority for the City. It also has numerous responsibilities and ownerships which lie beyond the City's boundaries.

The Latin motto of the City of London is "Domine dirige nos", which translates as "Lord, guide us".

Text B Landmarks in London

It is hardly surprising that England's capital city, home of the Royal family, is **crammed** full of **spectacular** landmarks and monuments. Famous throughout the world, many of these date back several hundreds of years and are in **remarkable** condition. Here are some of the top landmarks to visit.

1. The massive **White Tower** is a **typical** example of Norman military architecture, whose influence was felt throughout the kingdom. It was built on the Thames by William the Conqueror to protect London and **assert** his power. **The Tower of London**—an imposing fortress with many layers of history, which has become one of the symbols of royalty—was built around the White Tower.

2. Disliked by most when constructed in 1894, **the Tower Bridge** has become a symbol of London. The Tower Bridge, named after its two impressive towers, is one of London's best known landmarks. This Victorian Bridge is now more than 100 years old. Completed in 1894, the middle of the bridge can be raised to **permit** large vessels to pass the Tower Bridge. It used to be raised about 50 times a day, but nowadays it is only raised 4 to 5 times a week. The bridge is 60 meters (197 ft) long and its towers rise to a height of 43 meters. From the top of the towers, you have a great view on the center of London. You can also visit the inside of the tower, where you can **observe** the **original** mechanism used to raise the bridge.

3. The Palace of Westminster is better known as **the Houses of Parliament** and is one of London's best known monuments and also one of the city's finest Victorian buildings. It is best viewed from the south side of the river, where it has been painted by many **renowned** artists, including Monet and Turner.

4. Westminster Abbey is one of Europe's finest **Gothic** buildings and the scene of many **coronations**, marriages and burials of British monarchs. It dates back to the 11th century.

5. Buckingham Palace is over 300 years old and is the official London residence of Her Majesty Queen Elizabeth II, serving as both home and office. It is open to the public from mid-August until the end of September.

(To be continued)

After You Read

Knowledge Focus
1. **Fill in the blanks according to the geographical knowledge you have learned in the texts above.**
   (1) The city of London is often referred to as the City or as _____, as it is almost exactly one square mile in area. These terms are also often used as metonyms for the United Kingdom's _____ services industry.
   (2) Greater London or London covers the City of London and _____ London boroughs.
   (3) The City of London is still part of London's city center, but apart from financial services, most of London's metropolitan functions are centered on _____.
   (4) The River Thames crosses London from _____ to _____.
   (5) _____, named after its two impressive towers, is one of London's best known landmarks.
   (6) _____ was built on the Thames by William the Conqueror to protect London and assert his power.
   (7) _____, the Anglican Church, is one of Europe's finest Gothic buildings.
   (8) _____ is the official London residence of Her Majesty Queen Elizabeth II,

serving as both home and office.

2. **Write T in the brackets if the statement is true and write F if it is false.**
   (1) Greater London was created in 1965 and covers the City of London and 32 London boroughs. (　)
   (2) The Thames is a serene river, and London is invulnerable to flooding. (　)
   (3) The City of London is the historic core of London around which, along with Westminster, the modern conurbation grew. (　)
   (4) The Tower Bridge is raised about 50 times a day nowadays. (　)
   (5) The Palace of Westminster is better known as the Houses of Parliament and is one of London's best known monuments and also one of the city's finest Victorian buildings. (　)
   (6) Buckingham Palace is the official London residence of Her Majesty Queen Elizabeth II, serving as both home and office. (　)

Language Focus

1. **Fill in the blanks with the proper form of the phrases below.**

by far	present no obstacle to	be referred to as	deal with
due to	have responsibilities for	along with	expect...to

   (1) The Greater London region has _____ the highest GDP per capita in the United Kingdom.
   (2) It is the historic core of London around which, _____ Westminster, the modern conurbation grew.
   (3) It is often _____ just the City or as the Square Mile, as it is almost exactly one square mile (2.6 km²) in area.
   (4) The City is governed by the City of London Corporation, which _____ a local authority, such as being the police authority for the City.
   (5) These hills _____ the growth of London from its origins as a port on the north side of the river, and therefore London is roughly circular.
   (6) The threat has increased over time _____ a slow but continuous rise in high water level by the slow "tilting" of Britain caused by post-glacial rebound.
   (7) In 1974, a decade of work began on the construction of the Thames Barrier across the Thames at Woolwich to _____ this threat.
   (8) While the barrier _____ function as designed until roughly 2030, concepts for its future enlargement or redesign are already being discussed.

2. **Fill in the blanks with the appropriate form of the words in the brackets.**
   (1) The City employs 340,000 _____ (profession) workers, mainly in the financial sector, who _____ (commuter) on a _____ (day) basis.
   (2) Greater London is the top-level _____ (administrate) _____ (subdivide) covering London, England.
   (3) Its primary geographical feature is the Thames, a _____ (navigate) river.

(4) London has grown from its origins as a port on the north side of the river, and therefore London is _____ (rough) _____ (circle).

(5) Many of the highest points in London are located in the suburbs or on the boundaries with _____ (adjacency) counties.

(6) The Thames is a _____ (tide) river, and London is _____ (vulnerability) to flooding.

(7) While the barrier is expected to function as designed until roughly 2030, concepts for its future _____ (enlarge) or redesign are already being discussed.

(8) Buckingham Palace is best viewed from the south side of the river, where it has been painted by many _____ (renown) artists, including Monet and Turner.

(9) Westminster Abbey is the scene of many _____ (coronate), _____ (marry) and _____ (bury) of British monarchs.

(10) The shores of the Thames River reached five times their current _____ (wide) at high tide. Since the Victorian era the Thames River has been extensively _____ (embankment), and many of its London tributaries now flow underground.

3. **Fill in the blanks with the proper prepositions and adverbs that collocate with the neighboring words.**

(1) Many of the highest points in London are located _____ the suburbs or _____ the boundaries with adjacent counties.

(2) The Thames was once a much broader, shallower river _____ extensive marshlands; _____ high tide, its shores reached five times their current width.

(3) The City of London is a geographically small city _____ Greater London, England.

(4) These terms are also often used _____ metonyms _____ the United Kingdom's financial services industry, which is principally based there.

(5) Apart _____ financial services, most of London's metropolitan functions are centered _____ the West End.

(6) The City employs 340,000 professional workers, mainly in the financial sector, who commute _____ a daily basis—making the area's transport system extremely busy _____ certain peak times.

(7) The Latin motto of the City of London is "Domine dirige nos", which translates _____ "Lord, guide us".

(8) The White Tower was built _____ the Thames _____ William the Conqueror to protect London and assert his power.

4. **Correct the mistakes in the verb tenses in the following sentences, if there are any.**

(1) The administrative area was created in 1965 and covered the City of London and 32 London boroughs.

(2) Since the Victoria era it had been extensively embanked, and many of its London tributaries now flow underground.

(3) While the barrier is expected to function as designed until roughly 2030, concepts for its future enlargement or redesign are already discussed.

(4) The City's boundaries remained almost constant since the Middle Ages, and hence it is now only a tiny part of the much larger London metropolis.

(5) Disliked by most when constructed in 1894, the Tower Bridge becomes a symbol of London.

(6) The bridge, which dated from 1688, needs repairing.

(7) I hoped to see here off at the station, but I had been too busy.

(8) Next Monday, she has been in China for three years.

Comprehensive Work

1. **Pair Work**: Discuss the following cartoons with your partner.

Cartoon 1

(1) What is Cartoon 1 about?
(2) Who are the people and what are they doing?
(3) What's the point of this cartoon?

Cartoon 2

In Cartoon 2, there are two _____, who think London has changed a bit since their last visit because _____ has changed from a mechanical clock to a _____ clock.

Cartoon 3

(1) Where is it?
(2) What is happening?
(3) What is its point?

2. **Solo Work**: Surf the Internet or go to the library for relevant information. Compare and contrast Beijing in terms of their locations, culture, buildings, etc. Write a composition of about 300 words, illustrating their strengths and weaknesses and their future.

Read More

Text C   **More Landmarks**

(Continued)

Read the passage quickly. Find the landmark that each statement is about and fill in the blanks with the proper form of the words in the brackets.

(1) It is a giant _____ (observe) wheel located in the Jubilee Gardens on the South Bank.

(2) Its huge and elegant dome _____ (domination) the skyline of the City and gives _____ (stun) views over London.

(3) It opened in 1753 and has _____ (proud) itself on remaining free for all that time.

(4) It is the terraced house and has been the _____ (reside) of the Prime Minister.

(5) It cost around £750 million to build and was the centerpiece of the UK's millennium _____ (celebrate).

6. **Big Ben**, the enormous clock stands high above the Houses of Parliament and is named after the thirteen-ton main bell that **strikes** every hour.

7. A recent but already very popular tourist attraction is **the London Eye**, a giant observation wheel located in the Jubilee Gardens on the South Bank. The 135-meter tall structure was built as part of London's **millennium** celebrations.

8. **Trafalgar Square** is a square in London, England that **commemorates** the Battle of Trafalgar (1805), a British naval victory of the Napoleonic Wars. One of London's grandest architectural set pieces, Trafalgar Square was designed in 1820 by John Nash. As one of the few large public squares in the city, it has been a popular tourist attraction and the main focus of political **demonstrations** for over a century.

9. **Piccadilly Circus** got its name from the ruffs or "pickadills" worn by the dandies who used to **promenade** here in the late 17th century. Always busy with traffic, it is most famous for its massive **illuminated**, **animated** billboards.

10. **St. Paul's Cathedral** is one of the world's most famous cathedrals. It was designed by Sir Christopher Wren and built between 1675 and 1708 to **replace** the **previous** cathedral destroyed in the Great Fire of London in 1666. The huge and elegant dome dominates the skyline of the City and gives stunning views over London.

11. **The British Museum** opened in 1753 and has **prided** itself **on** remaining free for all that time. The British Museum **houses** more than an **incredible** 7 million objects and it would probably take a week to see everything. The

collection of Egyptian and Greek antiquities are without a doubt amongst the largest and best known in the world.

12. **Hyde Park** is a London Royal Park which Henry VIII acquired in 1536 (it had been owned by the monks of Westminster Abbey before that). It has a large area of open space in the city centre of 630 acres and a perimeter of 4 miles. It has the memorials at Marble Arch at the east side and Kensington Palace at the west. Also within its environs is the Albert Memorial, Queen Victoria's monument to her husband. The Serpentine Lake is popular for boating, sailing and even bathing. To the south of the Serpentine runs Rotten Row, the fashionable riding track through the park. While up by Speaker's Corner at Marble Arch you can hear Britons exercise their right to free speech. There may be a dozen or more at any one time, each standing on a soap box, and **spouting** (usually) **controversial** views, strongly held on any topic you can think of—religion, politics, fox hunting, trade unions, Europe, tourists.

13. Touted as "London's favorite tourist attraction", the statues at **Madame Tussaud's Wax Museum** have been **thrilling** visitors since Tussaud opened her first **permanent** exhibit in 1835.

14. **The Regent's Park** is the largest grass area for sports in Central London and offers a wide variety of activities, as well as an Open Air Theatre, the London Zoo and many cafes and restaurants.

15. One of London's most famous addresses is **No. 10 Downing Street**, the **terraced** house that has been the residence of the Prime Minister since it was presented to Sir Robert Walpole, Britain's first Prime Minister, by George II in 1732.

16. **London's Millennium Dome** cost around £750 million to build and was the centerpiece of the UK's millennium celebrations. It was built in Greenwich as this is where the concept of a central time was invented—Greenwich Mean Time (GMT).

Proper Nouns

Addington Hills 阿丁顿山
Berkshire 伯克郡
Big Ben 大本钟
Buckingham Palace 白金汉宫

GDP per capita 人均国内生产总值
Greenwich Mean Time (GMT) 格林威治标准时间
Hyde Park 海德公园
Kensington palace 肯辛顿宫

London's Millennium Dome 千年穹顶
Madame Tussaud's Wax Museum 杜莎夫人蜡像馆
Marble Arch 大理石拱门
Mary Le Bow 圣玛丽·勒·博教堂
No. 10 Downing Street 唐宁街10号
Parliament Hill 议会山
Piccadilly Circus 皮卡迪利广场
Primrose Hill 普林姆罗斯山
Pudding Lane 布丁巷
Rotten Row 国王路
Speaker's Corner 演讲角
St. Paul's Cathedral 圣保罗大教堂
Surrey 萨里郡
Sword of State 御剑
the Albert Memorial 阿尔伯特纪念堂
the British Museum 大英博物馆
the City of London 伦敦市（伦敦金融城）
the City of London Corporation 伦敦市法团（伦敦金融城公司）
the City of Westminster 威斯敏斯特市
the Houses of Parliament 议会大厦
the Jubilee Gardens 银禧花园
the London Eye 伦敦眼
the Palace of Westminster 威斯敏斯特宫
the Regent's Park 摄政公园
the Serpentine Lake 蛇形湖
the Square Mile 一平方英里（伦敦金融城别称）
the Tower Bridge（伦敦）塔桥
the Tower of London 伦敦塔
the Victorian era 维多利亚时代
the White Tower 白塔
Trafalgar Square 特拉法加广场
Turner（William Turner）威廉·透纳（著名英国风景画家）
West End 伦敦西区
Westerham Heights 韦斯特勒姆
Westminster 威斯敏斯特
Westminster Abbey 威斯敏斯特教堂/西敏寺
Woolwich 伍尔维奇

For Fun

Websites to visit

http://en.wikipedia.org/wiki/Greater_London

  This is a webpage about Greater London, on which you can find information on its status, politics, history, statistics, environment, education, etc.

http://en.wikipedia.org/wiki/City_of_London

  This is a webpage about the City of London, on which you can read information on its history, financial industry, local government, education, gardens, etc.

http://www.woodlands-junior.kent.sch.uk/customs/questions/london/buildings.htm

  This is a webpage about the famous buildings and landmarks in London, on which you can read brief introductions to the Tower of London, Westminster Abbey, the House of Parliament, St. Paul's Cathedral, the Monument, etc.

http://www.visitlondon.com/people/family/

  This is a website of London for kids, on which you can find a lot of interesting information about it.

Book to read

London by Edward Rutherfurd

  London is Edward Rutherfurd's third enormous volume of historical fiction. As with his previous works, London traces the history of a single location throughout its history by examining the interlinked lives of several families in Mitcheneresque manner. Although linked, each chapter of London can be read as a novel on its own.

Despite the rises and falls of the families Ducket, Silversleeves, Bull, Barnikal, Carpenter, Meredith and Penny, the real protagonist of the book is the city of London itself. Interspersed with the stories of the lives of his characters, Rutherfurd examines the life of London. This is, at once, both London's strength and weakness. Rutherfurd's history lessons give a concise lesson into the society, politics and culture, not only of London, but of England in general for the periods he explores.

Movies to see

Oliver Twist (2005)

Roman Polanski directs the classic Charles Dickens story of a young orphan boy who gets involved with a gang of pickpockets in 19th Century London. Abandoned at an early age, Oliver Twist is forced to live in a workhouse lorded over by the awful Mr. Bumble, who cheats the boys of their meager rations. Desperate yet determined, Oliver makes his escape to the streets of London. Penniless and alone, he is lured into a world of crime by the sinister Fagin—the mastermind of a gang of pint-sized pickpockets. Oliver's rescue by the kindly Mr. Brownlow is only the beginning of a series of adventures that lead him to the promise of a better life.

Lock, Stock and Two Smoking Barrels (1998)

It is a 1998 British crime film directed and written by Guy Ritchie. Four London working class stiffs pool their money to put one in a high stakes card game, but things go wrong and they end up owing half a million pounds and having one week to come up with the cash. In order to pay off his debts, he and his friends decide to rob a small-time gang who happen to be operating out of the flat next door.

Song to enjoy

London Bridge Is Falling Down

"London Bridge Is Falling Down" is a well-known traditional nursery rhyme which is found in different versions all over the world. The main verse is:

London Bridge Is falling down,
Falling down, Falling down.

London Bridge Is falling down,

My fair lady.

The rhyme is often used in a children's singing game, which exists in a wide variety of forms, with additional verses. The most common is that two players make an arch while the others pass through in single file. The arch is then lowered at the song's end to "catch" a player.

London bridge is falling down,
falling down, falling down.
London bridge is falling down,
my fair lady.

Build it up with iron bars,
iron bars, iron bars.
Build it up with iron bars,
my fair lady.

Iron bars will bend and break,
bend and break, bend and break.
Iron bars will bend and break,
my fair lady.

Build it up with silver and gold,
silver and gold, silver and gold.
Build it up with silver and gold,
my fair lady.

Unit 6
The East of England

> Oxford gave the world marmalade and a manner, Cambridge science and a sausage.
> —Anonymous

Unit Goals

- To have a general idea of the geography of the East of England
- To be familiar with the geographical terms about the East of England
- To be able to introduce the East of England
- To be able to describe the city of Cambridge and the Broads
- To be able to compare and contrast the University of Oxford and Cambridge
- To be able to use "with + object + complement" more skillfully

Before You Read

1. _____ is a university town and the administrative centre of the county of Cambridgeshire, England. It is also at the heart of the high-technology centre known as _____.
2. To commemorate Xu Zhimo, an early 20th century Chinese poet, in July, 2008, a white marble stone has been installed at the back of King's College, University of _____, on which _____ is inscribed a verse from Xu's best-known poem, "Saying _____ to _____ Again".

3. The following are some fish you can find in the East of England. Can you match the names with the pictures?

herring *cod* *flatfish*

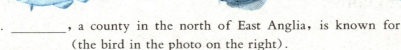

4. _____, a county in the north of East Anglia, is known for _____ (the bird in the photo on the right).

5. **Group Work:** Form groups of three or four students. Try to find, on the Internet or in the library, more information about the East of England, for example, its landscape, its economy, one of its towns and cities, which interests you most. Get ready for a 5-minute presentation in class.

Start to Read

Text A   **View of the East of England**

Location and Composition

  The East of England is based around the ancient kingdom of East Anglia, which was originally made up of Norfolk and Suffolk. These are now joined by Bedfordshire, Cambridgeshire, Essex and Hertfordshire to form the **bump** on England's eastern side. Besides the six counties, the East of England consists of four unitary authority areas—Luton, Peterborough, Southend-on-Sea and Thurrock. The area is directly to the north of London, and has **preserved** much of its **unspoilt** character, rural landscape, architecture and traditions.

Landscape

The countryside is predominately a low-lying and open area, containing a diversity of gentle landscapes—from flat fens (which support **intensive arable** farming) to chalk downland, heathland, man-made waterways, forest and ancient woodland. There is one National Park—The Broads of Norfolk and Suffolk; plus four 'Areas of Outstanding Natural Beauty'. These are the Norfolk and Suffolk Coasts, Dedham Vale, and the Chilterns.

The coastline covers 250 miles (402 kilometres), from the Wash (England's largest tidal estuary) to the wide expanse of the River Thames. With unspoilt beaches, **crumbling** cliffs, estuaries, shingle spits and Britain's best mudflats and saltmarshes, there are also seven key seaside destinations offering family fun and entertainment.

Important Towns and Cities

The region is home to Britain's oldest recorded town—Colchester, alongside the historic cities of Cambridge, Norwich and St. Albans. Traditional market towns and **picturesque** villages **abound**—home to outstanding examples of architecture—flint, thatch, timber-framed and weather-boarded buildings. Ipswich, Suffolk's chief town, is at the head of the river Orwell's estuary. Great Yarmouth in Norfolk is a holiday resort and a port. In the west, Newmarket attracts horse dealers to its annual auction.

1. Cambridge

Cambridge is one of the most well-known cities in the world because of the famous university there. Along with Oxford, Cambridge is one of Britain's ancient seats of learning. Today the centre of Cambridge is a mix of colleges, the normal life of a British town and the River Cam. In many ways their stories are similar, particularly the age-old conflict between town and gown. Cambridge can **namedrop** with the best of them, citing alumni such as Isaac Newton, John Milton, and Virginia Woolf. Cambridge continues to graduate many famous scientists such as physicist Stephen Hawking, author of *A Brief History of Time*.

In the 1990s, Cambridge became known as a high-tech outpost, or "a silicon fen", if you will. High-tech ventures continue to base themselves here to produce new software—start-up companies produce £2 billion a year in revenues. Even Bill Gates, in 1997, **financed** an £80 million research center here, **claiming** that Cambridge was becoming "a world center of advanced technology".

2. Norwich

Norwich still holds to its claim as the capital of East Anglia. Despite its **partial** industrialization, it is a charming and historic city. In addition to its cathedral, it has more than 30 medieval parish churches built of flint. It is also the most important shopping center in East Anglia and has a lot to offer in the way of entertainment and interesting hotels, many of them in its narrow streets and alleyways. A big open-air market is busy every weekday, with fruit, flowers, vegetables, and other goods sold from stalls with colored canvas roofs, by people from the local rural (farmland) areas. Unlike many cities, where department stores are very popular, Norwich has a variety of smaller specialist shops (shops that sell one specific thing), including the famous Mustard Shop. It sells mustard (a thick yellow or brown sauce that tastes spicy and is eaten cold in small amounts, especially with meat) and even has a museum.

Industry and Farming

Fishing is the region's most important industry. Cod, herring and flatfish are brought into Lowestoft in Suffolk, while at King's Lynn, situated on the relatively shallow bay of the Wash, the boats **trawl** for shellfish. Cromer is famous for its crabs. The Norfolk village of Oxford is known for its smokehouses, where meats and fish are preserved.

Essex has ship building at Tilbury, and an oil refinery near Canvey Island, but most of the country is farmland, with lots of fruit orchards.

East Anglia is a great agricultural region. Farmers grow cereals, sugar beet, fruit and vegetables, and they raise turkeys, sheep and cattle. Norfolk is well-known for its turkeys (they used to be marched to London in order to reach the market for Christmas, a journey which took three months) and now **boasts** the largest turkey farm in Europe.

After You Read

Knowledge Focus

1. Fill in the blanks according to the geographical knowledge you have learned in the text above.

　　(1) The East of England is made up of Suffolk, Norfolk, Essex, Hertfordshire,

Bedfordshire, _____ and four unitary authorities.
(2) The area of the East of England is directly to the _____ of London.
(3) The East of England houses one National Park—_____; plus four _____. These are the Norfolk and Suffolk Coasts; the Dedham Vale; and the Chilterns.
(4) The East of England is home to Britain's oldest recorded town—_____.
(5) Along with Oxford, _____ in East England is one of Britain's ancient seats of learning.
(6) _____ still holds to its claim as the capital of East Anglia.
(7) _____ is the most important industry in the East of England.
(8) East Anglia is a great _____ region. Farmers grow cereals, sugar beet, fruit and vegetables, and they raise turkeys, sheep and cattle.

2. **Write T in the brackets if the statement is true and write F if it is false.**
(1) The East of England is based around the ancient kingdom of East Anglia, which was originally made up of Norfolk and Suffolk. ( )
(2) The countryside in the East of England is predominately a low-lying and open area, containing only a single type of landscape. ( )
(3) In the East of England, here is one National Park—the Lake District National Park, plus four "Areas of Outstanding Natural Beauty". ( )
(4) The coastline of the East of England covers 250 miles from the Wash to the wide expanse of the River Severn. ( )
(5) Fishing is the most important industry in the East of England. ( )
(6) Norfolk is well-known for its turkeys and now boasts the largest turkey farm in Europe. ( )
(7) Norwich still holds to its claim as the capital of East Anglia. ( )

Language Focus
1. **Fill in the blanks with the proper form of the phrases below.**

| namedrop | attract...to | in addition to | be home to |
| be based around | be known for | continue to | hold to its claim |

(1) The East of England _____ the ancient kingdom of East Anglia, which was originally made up of Norfolk and Suffolk.
(2) The region _____ Britain's oldest recorded town—Colchester, alongside the historic cities of Cambridge, Norwich and St. Albans.
(3) In the west, Newmarket _____ horse dealers _____ its annual auction.
(4) Norwich still _____ as the capital of East Anglia.
(5) _____ its cathedral, it has more than 30 medieval parish churches built of flint.
(6) The Norfolk village of Oxford _____ its smokehouses, where meats and fish are preserved.
(7) High-tech ventures _____ base themselves here to produce new software.
(8) Cambridge can _____ with the best of them, citing alumni such as Isaac Newton, John Milton, and Virginia Woolf.

2. **Fill in the blanks with the appropriate form of the words in the brackets.**
   (1) The countryside is _____ (predomination) a low-lying and open area, containing a _____ (diverse) of gentle landscapes.
   (2) In East England, the flat fens support _____ (intensively) arable farming.
   (3) Bill Gates in 1997 claimed that Cambridge was becoming "a world center of _____ (advance) technology".
   (4) High-tech _____ (venturer) continue to base themselves here to produce new software.
   (5) Despite its _____ (part) industrialization, it is a charming and historic city.
   (6) King's Lynn is _____ (situation) on the relatively shallow bay of the Wash.

3. **Fill in the blanks with the proper prepositions and adverbs that collocate with the neighboring words.**
   (1) Ipswich, Suffolk's chief town, is _____ the head of the river Orwell's estuary.
   (2) _____ with Oxford, Cambridge is one of Britain's ancient seats of learning.
   (3) In many ways their stories are similar, particularly the age-old conflict _____ town and gown.
   (4) _____ many cities, where department stores are very popular, Norwich has a variety of smaller specialist shops (shops that sell one specific thing), including the famous Mustard Shop.
   (5) Cromer is famous _____ its crabs.
   (6) _____ the six counties, the East of England consists of four unitary authority areas.
   (7) In the 1990s, Cambridge became known _____ a high-tech outpost, or "a silicon fen", if you will.
   (8) A big open-air market is busy every weekday, with fruit, flowers, vegetables, and other goods sold from stalls _____ colored canvas roofs, by people _____ the local rural areas.

4. **Fill in the blanks with the proper form of the verbs in the brackets as the object complements of the preposition "with".**
   (1) A big open-air market is busy every weekday with fruit, flowers, vegetables, and other goods _____ (sell) with colored canvas roofs, by people from local rural areas.
   (2) I sat in my room for a few minutes with my eyes _____ (fix) on the ceiling.
   (3) He soon fell asleep with the lamp still _____ (burn).
   (4) He sat in the chair with his legs _____ (cross).
   (5) With such good cadres _____ (carry) out the Party's policy, we feel safe.
   (6) You can't leave here with the machine _____ (run).
   (7) I can't go out with you with so many books _____ (read).
   (8) With him _____ (take) charge of the task, I have no doubt of its success.

Comprehensive Work

1. **Pair Work**: Read the following famous poem about Cambridge by Xu Zhimo. And try to figure out the answers to the following questions with your partner:
   (1) Which pairs of sentences are rhymed? And how?
   (2) What landscape is there around Cambridge?
   (3) Why is it called "Cambridge"?
   (4) What emotion does the famous poet want to express?

再别康桥
徐志摩

轻轻的我走了,
正如我轻轻的来;
我轻轻的招手,
作别西天的云彩。
那河畔的金柳,
是夕阳中的新娘;
波光里的艳影,
在我的心头荡漾。
软泥上的青荇,
油油的在水底招摇;
在康河的柔波里,
我甘心做一条水草。
那树荫下的一潭,
不是清泉,是天上虹
揉碎在浮藻间,
沉淀着彩虹似的梦。
寻梦? 撑一支长篙,
向青草更青处漫溯,
满载一船星辉,
在星辉斑斓里放歌
但我不能放歌,
悄悄是别离的笙箫;
夏虫也为我沉默,
沉默是今晚的康桥!
悄悄的我走了,
正如我悄悄的来;
我挥一挥衣袖,
不带走一片云彩。

Saying Good-bye to Cambridge Again

Very quietly I take my leave
As quietly as I came here;
Quietly I wave good-bye
To the rosy clouds in the western sky.
The golden willows by the riverside
Are young brides in the setting sun;
Their reflections on the shimmering waves
Always linger in the depth of my heart.
The floating heart growing in the sludge
Sways leisurely under the water;
In the gentle waves of Cambridge
I would be a water plant!
That pool under the shade of elm trees
Holds not water but the rainbow from the sky;
Shattered to pieces among the duckweeds
Is the sediment of a rainbow-like dream?
To seek a dream? Just to pole a boat upstream
To where the green grass is more verdant;
Or to have the boat fully loaded with starlight
And sing aloud in the splendor of starlight.
But I cannot sing aloud
Quietness is my farewell music;
Even summer insects keep silence for me
Silent is Cambridge tonight!
Very quietly I take my leave
As quietly as I came here;
Gently I flick my sleeves
Not even a wisp of cloud will I bring away.

2. **Group Work**: Discuss, in groups of three or four students, the meaning of the quote at the very beginning of the unit. Choose a university you would like to go between Oxford and Cambridge if you have a great chance, and share your reasons with your

group members.

"Oxford gave the world marmalade and a manner, Cambridge science and a sausage."

The meaning: _____
_____
_____

Your choice (√):

University of Oxford ( )	
University of Cambridge ( )	

Your reasons: _____
_____

Read More

Text B New Stone Installed with China's Best-known Poem

Read the passage quickly and finish the multiple-choice questions below.

(1) The white marble stone has been installed _____.
   A. by the King   B. for the King   C. at the King's College

(2) Which of the following is true?
   A. Everyone agrees that Xu Zhimo is the greatest poet of the 20th century.
   B. Most educated Chinese know 'Saying Goodby to Cambridge Again,' and feel it is a very funny poem.
   C. Xu Zhimo died in his mid-thirties in an air crash.

(3) The underlined word "inscribe" in the last paragraph probably means _____.
   A. carve or etch into a surface
   B. make impossible
   C. set up

A white marble stone has been **installed** at the back of King's bearing a verse from the China's best-known poem. 'Saying Goodbye to Cambridge Again' is by **arguably** the greatest poet of the 20th century China, Xu Zhimo, and has an emotional place in many Chinese people's hearts.

Xu Zhimo wrote the poem on the King's College Backs, and it is thought that the golden willow of the poem is the tree that stands beside the bridge at King's, by which the stone has been installed. This poem is one which most educated Chinese know and many feel deeply moved by. It provides a bridge between China and Cambridge, and King's in particular. Many Chinese students think of this poem when leaving Cambridge.

Xu Zhimo died in 1931 at the young age of 36 in an air crash. He studied Politics and Economics during 1921-1922 and was associated with King's through Goldsworthy Lowes Dickinson. It was in Cambridge that, under the influence of poets such as Keats and Shelley, he began to write poetry.

A friend of Cambridge in China, Simon Jiang, arranged for the stone to be **inscribed** with the first two and last two lines of the poem and brought to Cambridge. It is made of white Beijing marble (the same stone used to construct the Forbidden City in Beijing) as a symbol of the continuing links between King's and China.

Proper Nouns

Bedfordshire 贝德福德郡
Bures 布尔兹
Cambridge 剑桥
Cambridgeshire 剑桥郡
Canvey Island 肯伟岛
Colchester 卡雀斯特镇
Constable Country 康斯特布尔之乡
Cromer 克罗默
Dedham Vale 戴德汉之谷
Essex 艾塞克斯郡
Goldsworthy Lowes Dickinson 哥兹沃西·洛兹·狄金森(英国知名作家、学者)
Great Yarmouth 大雅茅斯
Hertfordshire 赫特福德郡
Ipswich 伊普斯威奇
John Constable 约翰·康斯特布尔
John Milton 约翰·弥尔顿
King's Lynn 金斯林
Lowestoft 洛斯托夫特
Luton 卢顿
Newmarket 纽马克特

Norfolk 诺福克郡
Orford 奥福德
Peterborough 彼得伯勒
P. S. Shelley 雪莱(英国文学史上最有才华的抒情诗人之一)
Southend-on-Sea 绍森德
St. Albans 圣奥尔本斯
Suffolk 萨福克郡
Tilbury 蒂尔伯里
the Broads of Norfolk and Suffolk 湖区国家公园
the Chilterns 奇特恩斯山
the Forbidden City 故宫
the River Orwell 欧威尔河
the River Stour 斯陶尔河
the Victoria and Albelt Museum 英国维多利亚与阿尔伯特博物馆
the Wash 沃什湾
Thurrock 瑟罗克
Virginia Woolf 弗吉尼亚·伍尔芙
Xu Zhimo 徐志摩

For Fun

Websites to visit

http://en.wikipedia.org/wiki/Cambridge

　　This is a webpage about Cambridge, the university town in England, on which you can read such information as its history, geography, transport, politics, etc.

http://www.visiteastofengland.com/

　　This is the official online visitor's guide of the East of England, on which you can discover where to stay, exciting things to do, a comprehensive database of events, tourist information centers, regular news updates, etc.

Book to read

Ghostwalk by Rebecca Scott

　　Ghostwalk by Rebecca Stott is a story about Lydia Brooke, a woman who is asked to complete a nearly finished biography of Isaac Newton, written by the mother, Elizabeth Vogelsang, of her former lover, Cameron Brown. Set in Cambridge, the mother and author, is found drowned in a river near her cottage where she has been writing and researching the works of Newton and his ties to the practice and networks of alchemy. Her research reveals three murders in Cambridge at the time of Newton.

Movies to see

Chariots of Fire (1981)

　　It is the true story of two British track athletes competing in the 1924 Summer Olympics. One is a devout Scottish missionary who runs for God, the other is a Jewish student at Cambridge who runs for fame and to escape prejudice.

Peter's Friends (1992)

　　Seven friends in an acting troupe graduate from Cambridge University in 1982 and go their separate ways. Ten years later, Peter inherits a large estate from his father, and invites the rest of the gang to spend New Year's holiday with him. Many changes have taken place in the lives of all the friends assembled, but Peter has a secret that will shock them all.

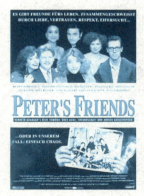

Song to enjoy

"Simple Gifts" (CD) by the King's Singers

    The King's Singers are a celebrated, long-lived, Grammy Award—winning British a cappella vocal ensemble. Their name recalls King's College in Cambridge, England, where the group was formed by six choral scholars in 1968. The group's popularity in the United Kingdom peaked in the 1970s and early 1980s. Thereafter they began to reach a wider audience in the U.S. Recently the current King's Singers have performed more regularly in the UK once again. In February 2009, their CD "Simple Gifts" won a Grammy Award for Best Classical Crossover album.

    Today the ensemble remains one of the world's most popular and sought-after vocal groups. They regularly travel worldwide for their performances, appearing in around 125 concerts each year, mostly in Europe, the U.S. and the Far East, having recently added the People's Republic of China to their list of touring territories.

Unit 7
East Midlands

> I can never decide whether my dreams are the result of my thoughts, or my thoughts the result of my dreams.
> —— D. H. Lawrence

Unit Goals

- To have a general idea of the geography of East Midlands
- To be familiar with the geographical terms about East Midlands
- To be able to introduce the East Midlands
- To be able to describe the Trent, the Peak Distrid and Notting ham
- To be able to understand the sentences with "see" whose subjects are periods of time or places

Before You Read

1. You have learned the Lake District in the county of _____ in England. Have you heard of the Peak District? What kind of landscape do you think it takes on?
2. _____ is the longest river in the UK; _____ the second longest; and _____ the third, which flows through the middle of England and which is used for drinking water, transport, power and leisure.
3. _____ is an archetypal figure in English folklore, whose story originates from medieval times, but who remains significant in popular culture where he is known for "robbing the rich to give to the poor" and fighting against injustice and

tyranny. His band includes a group of fellow outlawed yeomen—called his "_____". In popular culture, they are usually portrayed as living in _____ Forest, in _____.

4. **Group Work:** Form groups of three or four students. Try to find, on the Internet or in the library, more information about East Midlands, for example, its National Park, its economy, one of its towns and cities, which interests you most. Get ready for a 5-minute presentation in class.

Start to Read

Text A　　View of East Midlands

Location and Composition

The East Midlands is at the heart of Britain. It is made up of the five "shire" counties of Derbyshire, Nottinghamshire, Lincolnshire, Leicestershire and Northamptonshire plus four unitary authorities, namely Derby, Nottingham, Leicester, and Rutland.

Landscape

Most of the East Midlands is low-lying. The chalky Chiltern Hills lie along the southern boundary of this region. North of these in Northamptonshire lies the valley of the River Nene, running between two ridges of higher ground. Further north in Lincolnshire, the county consists of heathland with wolds (low hills) to the east, and marshland over in the west running towards the North Sea. The River Trent, Britain's third largest river, runs through Nottinghamshire to join the River Ouse and form the Humber.

The Peak District, a National Park, is in the northwest corner of the East Midlands. It is mostly in county of Derbyshire but **spills** over into **adjoining** counties.

Important Towns and Cities

The most important cities and towns are the ancient ones of Lincoln, Nottingham, and Northampton. The largest city and the generally recognized "capital" of the East Midlands is Nottingham.

1. Nottingham

"Notts", as Nottinghamshire is known, lies in the heart of the East Midlands. Its towns are rich in folklore or have **bustling** markets. Many famous people have come from Nottingham, notably those 13th-century outlaws from Sherwood Forest, Robin Hood and his Merry Men. It also was home to the romantic poet Lord Byron; you can visit his **ancestral** home at Newstead Abbey. D. H. Lawrence, author of *Sons and Lovers* and *Lady Chatterley's Lover*, was born in a tiny miner's cottage in Eastwood, which he later **immortalized** in his writings.

Nottingham was an important pre-Norman settlement guarding the River Trent, the gateway to the north of England. Followers of William the Conqueror arrived in 1068 to **erect** a fort here. The fort saw supporters of Prince John surrender to Richard the Lion-Hearted in 1194. Many other exploits occurred here—notably Edward III's capture of Roger Mortimer and Queen Isabella, the assassins of Edward II. From Nottingham, Richard III marched out with his men to face defeat and his own death at Bosworth Field in 1485.

With the **arrival** of the spinning jenny in 1768, Nottingham was **launched into** the forefront of the Industrial Revolution. It's still a center of industry and home base to many well-known British firms, turning out such products as John Player cigarettes, Boots pharmaceuticals, and Raleigh cycles.

Nottingham does not have many attractions, but it is a young and **vital** city, and is very **student-oriented** thanks to its two large universities. A look at one of the alternative newspapers or magazines freely **distributed** around town can connect you with the city's **constantly** changing nightlife scene.

2. Lincoln

The ancient city of Lincoln was the site of a Bronze Age settlement, and later, in the 3rd century, one of four provincial capitals of Roman Britain. In the Middle Ages, it was the center of Lindsey, a famous Anglo-Saxon kingdom. After the Norman Conquest, it grew **increasingly** important, known for its cathedral and castle. Its merchants grew rich by shipping wool directly to Flanders.

Much of the past remains in Lincoln today to **delight** visitors who wander past half-timbered Tudor houses, the Norman castle, and the towering Lincoln Cathedral. Medieval streets climbing the hillsides and cobblestones recreate the past. Lincoln, unlike other East Midlands towns such as Nottingham and Leicester, maintains somewhat of a country town atmosphere. But it also extends welcoming arms to tourists, the mainstay of its economy.

Industry and Farming

Nottingham has a worldwide **reputation** for its fine lace. There are also heavy industries and many power stations along the banks of the River Trent. Northampton is an important leather working centre. Leicester has shoe factories.

The rich, **peaty** fens have made the East Midlands one of England's most important arable lands. The region's farmers supply fruit and vegetables to local industries for freezing, canning and jam-making. Other crops include cereals and sugar beet. Shorthorn cows provide milk for making Stilton cheese, in Nottinghamshire.

After You Read

Knowledge Focus

1. **Fill in the blanks according to the geographical knowledge you have learned in the text above.**
   (1) The East _____ is at the heart of Britain. It includes the five "shire" counties of Derbyshire, _____, Lincolnshire, Leicestershire and Northamptonshire.
   (2) _____, Britain's third largest river, runs through Nottinghamshire to join the River Ouse and form the Humber.
   (3) _____, a National Park, is in the northwest corner of the East Midlands.
   (4) _____ is the largest city and the generally recognized "capital" of the East Midlands.
   (5) Nottingham was an important pre-Norman settlement guarding the River Trent, the gateway to _____.
   (6) Much of the past remains in _____ today to delight visitors who wander past half-timbered Tudor houses, the Norman castle, and the towering Lincoln Cathedral.
   (7) _____ is known worldwide for its fine lace.

2. Write T in the brackets if the statement is true and write F if it is false.

(1) Most of the East Midlands is low-lying. (　)

(2) The most important cities and towns in East Midlands are the ancient ones of Lincoln, Nottingham, Oxford. (　)

(3) The Peak District, a National Park, is in the northwest corner of the West Midlands. (　)

(4) Lincoln, and other East Midlands towns such as Nottingham and Leicester, maintain somewhat of a country town atmosphere. (　)

(5) Nottingham is still a center of industry and home base to many well-known British firms. (　)

(6) Many famous people have come from Nottingham, such as Robin Hood and his Merry Men, the romantic poet Lord Byron and D. H. Lawrence. (　)

Language Focus

1. Fill in the blanks with the proper form of the phrases below.

| at the heart of | launch...into | have a reputation | ship...to |
| spill over into | extend...to | provide...for | thanks to |

(1) The East Midlands is _____ Britain.

(2) It is mostly in county of Derbyshire but _____ adjoining counties.

(3) With the arrival of the spinning jenny in 1768, Nottingham was _____ the forefront of the Industrial Revolution.

(4) But it also _____ welcoming arms _____ tourists, the mainstay of its economy.

(5) Nottingham _____ for its fine lace.

(6) Shorthorn cows _____ milk _____ making Stilton cheese, in Nottinghamshire.

(7) Its merchants grew rich by _____ wool directly _____ Flanders.

(8) Nottingham does not have many attractions, but it is a young and vital city, and is very student-oriented _____ its two large universities.

2. Fill in the blanks with the appropriate form of the words in the brackets.

(1) The _____ (chalk) Chiltern Hills lie along the southern boundary of this East Midlands.

(2) The Peak District is mostly in county of Derbyshire but spills over into _____ (adjoin) counties.

(3) The towns in Nottinghamshire are rich in folklore or have _____ (bustle) markets.

(4) In Nottingham, tourists can visit Lord Byron's _____ (ancestor) home at Newstead Abbey.

(5) D. H. Lawrence was born in a tiny miner's cottage in Eastwood, which he later _____ (immortal) in his writings.

(6) Followers of William the Conqueror arrived in 1068 to _____ (erection) a

fort in Nottingham.
(7) Many other exploits occurred here—_____(notable) Edward III's capture of Roger Mortimer and Queen Isabella, the _____ (assassinate) of Edward II.
(8) With the _____ (arrive) of the _____ (spin) jenny in 1768, Nottingham was launched into the forefront of the Industrial Revolution.
(9) Nottingham is still a center of industry and home base to many well-known British firms, turning out such products as John Player cigarettes, Boots _____ (pharmacy), and Raleigh cycles.
(10) The newspapers or magazines freely _____ (distribution) around town can connect you with the city's _____ (constancy) changing nightlife scene.
(11) The ancient city of Lincoln was the site of a Bronze Age _____ (settle), and later, in the 3rd century, one of four _____ (province) capitals of Roman Britain.
(12) Lincoln also extends _____ (welcome) arms to tourists, the mainstay of its economy.
(13) Nottingham has a worldwide _____ (reputed) for its fine lace.
(14) The rich, _____ (peat) fens have made the East Midlands one of England's most important _____ (arability) lands.

3. **Fill in the blanks with the proper prepositions and adverbs that collocate with the neighboring words.**
    (1) It is made up _____ the five "shire" counties.
    (2) The chalky Chiltern Hills lie _____ the southern boundary of this region.
    (3) Its towns are rich _____ folklore or have bustling markets.
    (4) A look _____ one of the alternative newspapers or magazines freely distributed around town can connect you _____ the city's constantly changing nightlife scene.
    (5) The region's farmers supply fruit and vegetables _____ local industries _____ freezing, canning and jam-making.
    (6) Lawrence was born _____ a tiny miner's cottage in Eastwood, which he later immortalized _____ his writings.
    (7) It is still a center of industry and home base _____ many well-known British firms, turning _____ such products as John Player cigarettes, Boots pharmaceuticals, and Raleigh cycles.

4. **Translate the following sentence with the different forms of "see" into Chinese.**
    (1) The fort saw supporters of Prince John surrender to Richard the Lion-Hearted in 1194.
    (2) The stadium has seen many important football matches.
    (3) This old house has seen many better days.
    (4) 1998 saw several new ventures promoting online distance learning for both college- and graduate-level courses.
    (5) Mr. Frank has seen the economy of his town slashed by the uprising.

(6) The First Century saw the appearance of Christianity.

(7) Yesterday saw the resignation of the acting Interior Minister.

(8) He had worked with the General for three years and was sorry to see him go.

Comprehensive Work

1. **Solo Work**: Fill in the blanks according to the map below and the information you have got from the text.

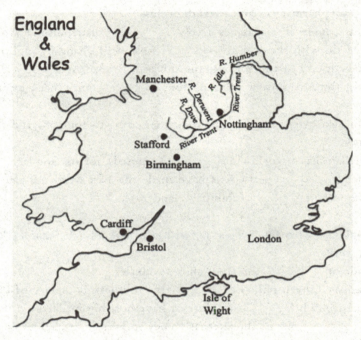

Here is a map of England and _____ (Scotland/Wales). The River Trent is 274 kilometres (171 miles) long. It is one of the major rivers of _____ (England/Wales). Its source is in Staffordshire. It flows through _____ (the East of England /the Midlands) until it joins the River _____ (Thames/Ouse) at Trent Falls to form the _____ (Wash/Humber) Estuary, which empties into the _____ (North/Irish) Sea.

2. **Pair Work**: Discuss, with your partner, the following questions about the cartoon.

(1) Where is it?

(2) What does the billboard tell to the tourists?

(3) What landscape do you think Nottinghamshire has?

3. **Solo Work**: Are there any famous people from your hometown? Write a poem, essay or lyrics, introducing (one of) them.

Read More

Text B　　Heroes in Nottinghamshire

Read the following passage quickly and fill in the blanks accordingly.

(1) D. H. Lawrence was born in Eastwood, _____ in 1885 and died in _____ in 1930. He has a _____ reputation, but he felt strongly attached to _____.

(2) Robin Hood, a world-famous outlaw in the tales, is a master _____ with a quick mind and mischievous sense of _____. He ambushes _____ travelers, fights _____ officials, and shares the spoils of his outlawry with _____, oppressed peasants.

(3) _____ was an English _____ and a leading figure in _____, whose fame rests not only on his writings, such as *Childe Harold's Pilgrimage* and _____, but also on his life, which featured _____ living, _____ love affairs, debts, separation, allegations of homosexuality and marital exploits.

D. H. Lawrence

"Life is ours to be spent, not to be saved." By D. H. Lawrence

D. H. Lawrence revolutionized the world of literature. But this controversial novelist came from **humble** beginnings—he was born in a small terraced house in Eastwood, Nottinghamshire in 1885. Now a museum, the house looks just as it did when Lawrence was a child.

The **inspirational** author of *Lady Chatterley's Lover* attended Nottingham High School and then Nottingham University. Today, a life-sized bronze statue of Lawrence lies within the University Park campus. Following his death in France in 1930, D. H. Lawrence's headstone was transported back to England. This is now on public **display** at Eastwood library.

Despite his international reputation he always felt strongly **attached to** Nottinghamshire, 'the country of my heart' and many of his novels are set around the Hidden Valleys area.

Many of the local scenes and sites have **inspired** his novels. Moorgreen inspired parts of *The White Peacock* and *Women in Love*. Felley Mill Farm and Pond, Underwood, are Strelley Mill in *The White Peacock* and Brinsley Colliery Headstocks pay tribute to the mine where his father worked.

Robin Hood

Tales of Robin Hood have been told for 700 years and our fascination with this world-famous outlaw continues into the 21st century. The romantic image of Robin Hood is of a medieval hooded figure in Lincoln Green, a master bowman with a quick mind and mischievous sense of humor. Dispossessed by greedy Norman overlords, he is forced to live beyond the law in the leafy depths of Sherwood, a royal hunting forest. From his forest lair he ambushes rich travelers, fights corrupt officials, and shares the spoils of his outlawry with poor, oppressed peasants.

Down the centuries this image has been elaborated and enlarged upon by literature, theatre and—more recently—film and TV shows. Many famous actors have played the people's hero. Some films have taken a less serious look at the time-honored tale, including a Walt Disney cartoon and a gangster style musical.

Lord Byron

George Gordon Byron, 6th Baron Byron, commonly known as Lord Byron, was an English poet and a leading figure in Romanticism. Among Lord Byron's best-known works are the narrative poems *Childe Harold's Pilgrimage* and *Don Juan*. The latter remained incomplete on his death. He is regarded as one of the greatest European poets and remains widely read and influential, both in the English speaking world and beyond.

Lord Byron's fame rests not only on his writings but also on his life, which featured extravagant living, numerous love affairs, debts, separation, allegations of homosexuality and marital exploits. He was famously described by Lady Caroline Lamb as "mad, bad, and dangerous to know".

Proper Nouns

All Saints' Church 诸圣教堂(北安普敦)
Bosworth Field 博斯沃思菲尔德战役
Brinsley Colliery Headstocks 布林斯利煤矿主轴箱
Bronze Age 铜器时代
Childe Harold's Pilgrimage《恰尔德·哈罗德游记》
Derby 德比市
Derbyshire 德比郡
D. H. Lawrence D. H. 劳伦斯
Don Juan《唐璜》
East Midlands 东米德兰地区(英格兰中东部)
Eastwood 伊斯特伍德镇(劳伦斯出生地)
Edward II 爱德华二世
Flanders 佛兰德斯(中世纪欧洲一伯爵领地)
Lady Caroline Lamb 卡罗琳·兰姆女士
Lady Chatterley's Lover《查特莱夫人的情人》
Leicester 莱斯特
Leicestershire 莱斯特郡
Lincoln Cathedral 林肯大教堂
Lincolnshire 林肯郡
Lindsey 林赛(王国)
Moorgreen 穆尔格林(诺丁汉郡一城市)

Newstead Abbey 纽斯泰德修道院(拜伦故居)
Northampton 北安普敦
Northamptonshire 北安普敦郡
Nottingham 诺丁汉
Nottinghamshire 诺丁汉郡
Prince John 约翰王子
Queen Isabella (西班牙)女皇伊莎贝拉
Richard III 理查三世
Richard the Lion-Hearted 狮心王理查(理查一世)
Robin Hood 罗宾汉
Roger Mortimer 罗杰·莫蒂默(第一代马奇伯爵)
Sherwood Forest 舍伍德森林
Sons and Lovers《儿子与情人》
Strelley Mill 斯特雷利磨坊
Stilton Cheese 斯提尔顿奶酪
the Guildhall 市政厅
the Humber 亨伯河口湾
the River Nene 宁河
the River Ouse 乌斯河
The White Peacock《白孔雀》
Women in Love《恋爱中的女人》

For Fun

Websites to visit

http://www.enjoyeastmidlands.com/

　　This is a website about the East Midlands, on which you can discover the treasures of Robin Hood, the Peak District National Park and more.

http://www.visitnottingham.com/

　　This is a website about Nottingham, on which you can experience the vibrant city life, beautiful countryside, traditional market towns, etc.

http://www.visitlincolnshire.com/

　　This is a website about Lincolnshire, on which you can find such information as places to visit, things to do, places to eat, etc.

Books to read

Supernatural Peak District by David Clarke

　　The Peak District is Britain's most popular national park with its miles of high moorland and unspoilt dales attracting millions of visitors every year. It is rich in folklore

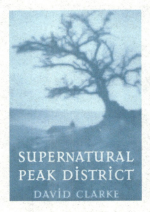
and traditions which stretch back to the dawn of history, with every village and hamlet having its own miscellany of strange happenings, from tales of headless horsemen to ghostly black dogs, boggarts and screaming skulls. Journalist and folklorist David Clarke has reached beyond the old legends by collecting personal experiences of the unexplained and documents all aspects of supernatural phenomena, from haunted lead-mines to stories of mysterious big cats, poltergeists and UFOs, using eye-witness accounts from residents and visitors. *Supernatural Peak District* takes the reader on a spine-chilling excursion through haunted Longdendale with its ghostly lights and spectral Roman legions to the Derwent Valley and its phantom Lancaster bomber that skims the waters of the Ladybower Reservoir on their first full moon of spring. For those venturing into the area by car, there are accounts of road ghosts including the cowled monk who patrols the Stocksbridge bypass and the ominous figure in black who guards the crossroads on the eerie moors. So, whether you are a seasoned ghost-hunter or simply a curious first-timer, this book will unveil a secret landscape beyond the tourist trails, just waiting to be explored.

The Adventures of Robin Hood by Marcia Williams

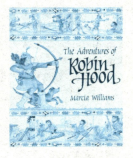

Told in lively comic-strip style, this book relates eleven colorful action-packed tales about Robin and his merry men. Read how Robin becomes an outlaw, gets a ducking from Little John and encounters a disguised Maid Marian in the forest; enjoy the stories of Much the Miller's Son, Friar Tuck, Allan-a-Dale, Sir Richard of Leigh and the golden arrow. Meet Robin's sworn enemy Sir Guy of Gisborne, witness his visit from King Richard and see Robin fire his final arrow.

Selected Poems of Lord Byron

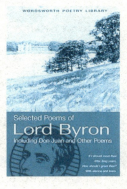

A legend in his lifetime, Lord Byron was the dominant influence on the Romantic Movement. The text of this edition, which contains nearly all of Byron's published poems together with the poet's own notes, was first published in *The Oxford Poets* in 1896, and has been reprinted numerous times.

Fredrick Page's text has been revised by John Jump, who has made a number of substantive corrections, and added to *Don Juan* the fragment of a seventeenth canto that was previously unavailable.

Movies to see
Robin Hood（1973）

It is an animated film produced by the Walt Disney Studios, first released in the United States on November 8, 1973.

The film retells the Robin Hood legend with animals for the characters. Robin Hood is an outlaw who starts to form a gang in Sherwood Forest to fight the injustices of the Sheriff of Nottingham, who levies unpayable taxes upon the people.

Fun and romance abounds as the swashbuckling hero of Sherwood Forest, and his valiant sidekick plot one daring adventure after another to outwit the greedy prince and his partner as they put the tax squeeze on the poor.

Robin Hood: Prince of Thieves (1991)

It is a 1991 adventure film directed. The film was marketed with the tagline "For the good of all men, and the love of one woman, he fought to uphold justice by breaking the law."

The film is about the adventures of Robin Hood after his return from the Crusades. With an indebted Moor by his side, Robin sets out to avenge his father's death and to save the peasants of Nottingham from their crafty, cunning sheriff.

Song to enjoy

(Everything I Do) I Do It for You
By Bryan Adams

It is a song co-written and performed by Bryan Adams, featured on his 1991 album "Waking up the Neighbours" and on the soundtrack for the film *Robin Hood: Prince of Thieves* (1991).

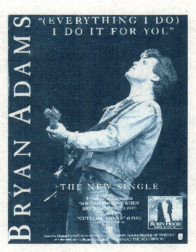

Look into my eyes—you will see
What you mean to me
Search your heart—search your soul
And when you find me there you'll search no more

Don't tell me it's not worth tryin' for
You can't tell me it's not worth dyin' for

You know it's true
Everything I do—I do it for you

Look into your heart—you will find
There's nothin' there to hide
Take me as I am—take my life
I would give it all—I would sacrifice

Don't tell me it's not worth fightin' for
I can't help it—there's nothin' I want more
Ya know it's true
Everything I do—I do it for you

There's no love—like your love
And no other—could give more love
There's nowhere—unless you're there

All the time—all the way

Oh—you can't tell me it's not worth tryin' for
I can't help it—there's nothin' I want more
I would fight for you—I'd lie for you
Walk the wire for you—ya I'd die for you

Ya know it's true
Everything I do—I do it for you

Unit 8
West Midlands

> England has two books, one which she has made and one which has made her: Shakespeare and the Bible.
> —Victor Hugo

Unit Goals

- To have a general idea of the geography of West Midlands
- To be familiar with the geographical terms about West Midlands
- To be able to introduce the West Midlands
- To be able to describe Birmingham and Coventry
- To be able to use the modal verbs more skillfully

Before You Read

1. Have you heard of a city whose reputation was forged as a powerhouse of the Industrial Revolution in England? It is a fact which led to its fame as "the _____ of the world" or the "city of a thousand _____". Where is it in the UK?
2. _____, widely regarded as the greatest writer in the English language and the world's preeminent dramatist, was born and raised in Stratford-upon-Avon, Warwickshire. _____, *Macbeth*, *Othello*, _____ are four of his greatest tragedies.

3. Peeping _____ is a person who, in the legend of _____, watched her during her ride through the ancient market town of _____ and was struck blind or dead. Today, Godiva Chocolatier is a manufacturer of premium chocolates and related products.

4. **Group Work**: Form groups of three or four students. Try to find, on the Internet or in the library, more information about West Midlands, for example, its National Park, its economy, one of its towns and cities, which interests you most. Get ready for a 5-minute presentation in class.

Start to Read

Text A View of West Midlands

Location and Composition

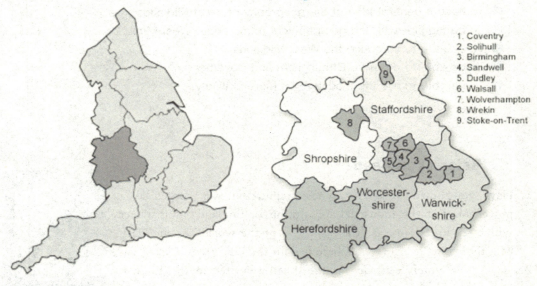

The West Midlands is located in the centre of Britain. It includes the counties of Herefordshire, Worcestershire, Shropshire, Staffordshire and Warwickshire as well as seven Metropolitan boroughs. The West Midlands region **represents** the heartland of Britain geographically, industrially, and economically. It contains the largest **concentration** of manufacturing and engineering companies in the UK. (The term "West Midlands", is also used for the much smaller West Midlands county.)

Landscape

The region is geographically diverse, from the urban central areas of the **conurbation** to the rural western counties of Shropshire and Herefordshire which border Wales. The longest river in the UK, the River Severn, **traverses** the region southeastwards, flowing through the county towns of Shrewsbury and Worcester, and the Ironbridge Gorge, a UNESCO World Heritage Site, as symbol of the Industrial Revolution. The region contains five Areas of Outstanding Natural Beauty (AONBs), including all of the Shropshire Hills, Malvern Hills and Cannock Chase, and parts of the Wye Valley and Cotswolds. The Peak District national park also **stretches into** the northern corner of Staffordshire.

Important Towns and Cities

In the heart of the West Midlands lies the city of Birmingham, a major centre of industry and the arts. Stratford-upon-Avon in Warwickshire is famous for the birthplace of the writer William Shakespeare. Hereford, Warick and Worcester are historic cities with many fine buildings.

1. Birmingham

England's second-largest city may **lay claim** fairly **to** the title "Birthplace of the Industrial Revolution". It was here that James Watt first used the steam engine with success to mine the Black Country. Watt and other famous 18th-century  members of the Lunar Society regularly met under a full moon in  the nearby Soho mansion of manufacturer Matthew Boulton. Together, Watt, Boulton, and other "lunatics", as Joseph Priestly, Charles Darwin, and Josiah Wedgwood cheerfully called themselves, launched the revolution that **thrust** England and the world **into** the modern era.

Today, this **brawny**, **unpretentious** metropolis still bears some of the scars of industrial **excess** and the **devastation** of the Nazi Luftwaffe bombing during World War II. But an energetic building boom has occurred recently, and Brummies have **nurtured** the city's modern rebirth by **fashioning** Birmingham **into** a convention city that **hosts** 80% of all trade exhibitions in the country.

Birmingham has worked **diligently** in recent decades to overcome the **blight** of over-industrialization and poor urban planning. New areas of green space and the city's cultivation of a first-rate symphony and ballet company, as well as art galleries and museums, have all made Birmingham more appealing.

Though not an obvious tourist highlight, Birmingham serves as a gateway to England's north. With more than 1 million inhabitants, Birmingham has a **vibrant** nightlife and restaurant scene. Its three universities, 2,428 hectares (6,000 acres) of parks and nearby pastoral sanctuaries, and **restored** canal walkways also offer welcome quiet places.

2. Coventry

Coventry has long been noted in legend as the ancient market town through which Lady Godiva took her famous ride in the **buff** (giving rise to the term Peeping Tom). A real Lady Godiva actually existed in the 11th century and was the wife of Leofric, earl of Mercia, one of England's most powerful noblemen. She was a **benefactor** to the poor and **urged** her husband **to** reduce their tax burden, which he agreed to do at a price. He made her a bet. If she would ride naked through Coventry market at midday, he would **in return** abolish all local taxes. On the appointed day, she rode naked through the market, unashamed of her **nudity**, and the taxes were duly removed. As such, she rode into legend, and that is the naked truth.

Coventry today is a Midlands industrial city. The city was partially destroyed by German bombers during World War II, but the **restoration** is **miraculous**.

Industry

Birmingham is home to so many different industries that it was nicknamed the "city of 1001 trades". Trade has been an important part of life in Birmingham for 800 years. Coventry was the birth place of the bicycle and has a large car industry. It is also famous for its aircraft, which is why it suffered such heavy bombing during World War II. Stoke-on-Trent is the centre of the ceramics industry. Wedgwood, Spode and Royal Doulton

all have factories here. Together with nearby towns, it makes up an industrial area known as "the Potteries". Worcester is also known for its fine porcelain.

After You Read

Knowledge Focus

1. **Fill in the blanks according to the geographical knowledge you have learned in the text above.**
   (1) The West Midlands is located in the centre of _____.
   (2) The West Midlands is home to five _____ and part of _____ National Park.
   (3) In the heart of the West Midlands lies the city of _____, a major centre of industry and the arts.
   (4) _____ in Warwickshire is famous for the birthplace of William Shakespeare.
   (5) It was in _____ that James Watt first used the steam engine with success to mine _____.
   (6) _____ was nicknamed the "city of 1001 trades".
   (7) _____ has long been noted in legend as the ancient market town through which Lady Godiva took her famous ride in the buff.
   (8) _____ was the birth place of the bicycle and has a large car industry. It is also famous for its aircraft, which is why it suffered such heavy bombing during _____.

2. **Write T in the brackets if the statement is true and write F if it is false.**
   (1) "West Midlands" is the name of a county as well as the name of a region. ( )
   (2) Birmingham is a major centre of industry and the arts. ( )
   (3) Stratford-upon-Avon in Shropshire is famous for the birthplace of the writer William Shakespeare. ( )
   (4) Birmingham is the second largest city in the UK. ( )
   (5) Coventry borders Birmingham. ( )
   (6) Lady Godiva took her famous ride in the buff through the ancient town market of Coventry. ( )
   (7) Nobody watched Lady Godiva during her naked ride because they knew she was helping to reduce the tax burden. ( )
   (8) Stoke-on-Trent in West Midlands is the centre of the ceramics industry. ( )

3. **Pair Work:** Discuss the following questions about the West Midlands with your partner.
   (1) Where is Birmingham? Is it a large city? What is it famous for?
   (2) Where is Coventry? Why is Lady Godiva so famous there?
   (3) Where are Stratford-upon-Avon and Stoke-on-Trent? What are they well-known for respectively?

Language Focus

1. **Fill in the blanks with the proper form of the phrases below.**

bear the scars of	serve as	in return
fashion...into	launch the revolution	urge...to
lay claim to	unashamed of	

(1) England's second-largest city may _____ the title "Birthplace of the Industrial Revolution".
(2) The "lunatics" _____ that thrust England and the world into the modern era.
(3) Though not an obvious tourist highlight, Birmingham _____ a gateway to England's north.
(4) She was a benefactor to the poor and _____ her husband _____ reduce their tax burden, which he agreed to do at a price.
(5) He made her a bet. If she'd ride naked through Coventry market at midday, he would _____ abolish all local taxes.
(6) On the appointed day, she rode naked through the market, _____ her nudity, and the taxes were duly removed.
(7) Brummies have nurtured the city's modern rebirth by _____ Birmingham _____ a convention city.
(8) Today, Birmingham still _____ industrial excess and the devastation of the Nazi Luftwaffe bombing during World War II.

2. **Fill in the blanks with the appropriate form of the words in the brackets.**

(1) The West Midlands represents the heartland of Britain _____ (geography), industrially, and _____ (economy).
(2) The West Midlands contains the largest _____ (concentrate) of manufacturing and engineering companies in the UK.
(3) Watt and other famous members of the Lunar Society _____ (regular) met under a full moon in the nearby Soho mansion of _____ (manufacture) Matthew Boulton.
(4) Today, this brawny, _____ (pretension) metropolis still bears some of the scars of industrial excess and the _____ (devastate) of the Nazi Luftwaffe bombing during World War II.
(5) Birmingham has worked _____ (diligence) in recent decades to overcome the blight of over-industrialization and poor urban planning.
(6) New areas of green space and the city's _____ (cultivate) of a first-rate symphony and ballet company have all made Birmingham more _____ (appeal).
(7) With more than 1 million _____ (inhabit), the city of Birmingham has a _____ (vibrancy) nightlife and restaurant scene.
(8) Godiva was a _____ (benefaction) to the poor and urged her husband to reduce their tax burden, which he agreed to do at a price.
(9) On the appointed day, she rode _____ (nake) through the market, unashamed of her _____ (nude), and the taxes were _____ (due) removed.
(10) Coventry was _____ (part) destroyed by German bombers during World War II, but the _____ (restore) is _____ (miracle).

3. **Fill in the blanks with the proper prepositions and adverbs that collocate with the neighboring words.**
   (1) The West Midlands is located _____ the centre of Britain.
   (2) The term "West Midlands", is also used _____ the much smaller West Midlands county.
   (3) It was here that James Watt first used the steam engine _____ success to mine the Black Country.
   (4) Birmingham has worked diligently _____ recent decades.
   (5) Coventry has long been noted _____ legend as the ancient market town through which Lady Godiva took her famous ride _____ the buff.
   (6) _____ the appointed day, she rode naked through the market.
   (7) He agreed to reduce the tax burden _____ a price.
   (8) Together _____ nearby towns, Stoke-on-Trent makes up an industrial area known _____ "the Potteries".

4. **Fill in the blanks with the modal verbs.**
   (1) England's second largest city _____ lay claim fairly to the title "Birthplace of the Industrial Revolution".
   (2) Her husband made her a bet. If she _____ ride naked through Coventry market at midday, he would in return abolish all local taxes.
   (3) This is not only incorrect but _____ cause offence to people from other parts of the UK.
   (4) Everywhere are the hints for the age-old conflict between town and gown. Cambridge _____ namedrop with the best of them, citing alumni such as Isaac Newton, John Milton and Virginia Woolf.
   (5) _____ you have a pleasant trip!
   (6) There's nothing to do, so I _____ as well watch TV.
   (7) They ought to go home, _____ they?
   (8) —Must I clean all the rooms?
      —No, you _____ .

Comprehensive Work

1. **Group Work:** Discuss the following questions about the cartoon within a group of three or four students.
   (1) What are displayed in the cartoon?
   (2) Where is it? Why? So what kind of city is it?

2. **Solo Work**: Rewrite the whole story of Lady Godiva in the form of a short story or a poem. And send it to one of your former high school friends.

Text B Stratford-Upon-Avon

Select the probable meaning of the underlined words in the passage.

(1) overrun _____
   A. travel in large numbers
   B. run too many markets
   C. injure with a vehicle

(2) make a buck _____
   A. earn money   B. worship   C. force...out

(3) dwindle _____
   A. become larger   B. become smaller   C. come back

(4) devoid _____
   A. not lacking   B. lacking   C. filled

Crowds of tourists <u>overrun</u> this market town on the River Avon during the summer. In fact, today, Stratford aggressively hustles its Shakespeare connection—everybody seems to be in business to <u>make a buck</u> off the Bard. However, the throngs <u>dwindle</u> in winter, when you can at least walk on the streets and seek out the places of genuine historic interest.

Aside from the historic sites, the major draw for visitors is the Royal Shakespeare Theatre, where Britain's foremost actors perform during a long season that lasts from April to October. Other than the theater, Stratford is rather <u>devoid of</u> any rich cultural life, and you may want to rush back to London after you have seen the literary pilgrimage sights and watched a production of *Hamlet*. But Stratford-upon-Avon is also a good center for trips to Warwick Castle, Kenilworth Castle, and Coventry Cathedral.

Proper Nouns

Birmingham 伯明翰
Charles Darwin 查尔斯·达尔文
Coventry Cathedral 考文垂大教堂
Dudley 达德利
Hamlet《哈姆莱特》
Hereford 赫特福德
Herefordshire 赫特福德郡
James Watt 詹姆斯·瓦特
Joseph Priestly 约瑟夫·普利斯特
Josiah Wedgwood 乔什瓦·韦奇伍德
Kenilworth Castle 凯尼尔沃思古堡
Lady Godiva 戈黛娃夫人
Leofric, earl of Mercia 麦西亚伯爵利奥夫里克
Matthew Boulton 马修·博尔顿
Meriden 梅里登
Nazi Luftwaffe（第二次世界大战中的）纳粹德国空军
Peeping Tom 窥视者
Royal Doulton 皇家道尔顿公司
Sandwell 桑德维尔
Shrewsbury 什鲁斯伯里
Shropshire 什罗普郡
Solihull 索里赫尔

Spode 斯波德陶瓷公司
Staffordshire 斯塔福德郡
Stoke-on-Trent 特伦特河畔斯托克
the Bard (of Avon) 艾冯河的吟游诗人(莎士比亚的别称)
the Cannock Chase 坎诺克蔡斯
the Cotswolds 科茨沃尔兹(又译:科茨沃尔德丘陵地带)
the Ironbridge Gorge 铁桥峡谷
the Lunar Society 月协会(又译:月亮社、月圆会)
the Malvern Hills 马文山
the Peak District National Park 峰区国家公园
the Royal Shakespeare Theatre 皇家莎士比亚剧院
the Shropshire Hills 什罗普郡山
the Wye Valley 渭谷河畔
Walsall 沃尔索尔
Warick 华威(又译:沃里克)
Warwick Castle 华威城堡(又译:沃里克城堡)
Warwickshire 华威郡(又译:沃里克郡)
Wedgwood 韦奇伍德公司
Wolverhampton 伍尔弗汉普顿
Worcester 伍斯特
Worcestershire 伍斯特郡

For Fun

Websites to visit

http://www.visitbirmingham.com/

This is a website about visiting Birmingham, on which you can read its art and culture, nightlife, sports, etc.

http://www.bclm.co.uk/

This is a website about the Black Country Living Museum, on which you can read all kinds of information about the Black Country and have a "real" experience of visiting it.

Books to read

Horrible Histories: Stratford-upon-Avon by Terry Deary

It is about the birthplace of the brilliant bard William Shakespeare. A quaint and cute tourist town today, Shakespeare's Stratford was far from pleasant and Terry Deary reveals the civil war struggles and brutal beheadings that made its history so horrible. Readers can explore all the horrible highlights of the town using the frightful fold-out map, including spooky Sheep Street, home of an awful axeman, a weird witch and possibly the most haunted house in England.

Coventry: A Novel by Helen Humphreys

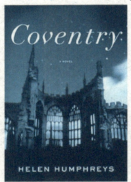

Humphreys's lethargic latest depicts the intertwining lives of two British women during the world wars. Harriet and Maeve meet on the streets of Coventry, England, in 1914. Both are of troubled mind: Harriet's husband has just left for the battlegrounds of France, and Maeve cannot shake a deep sense of loneliness. The women share laughs on a bus ride, but afterwards their lives continue on different paths. Harriet's husband, Owen, goes missing (and is presumed killed) in action, and Harriet spends the next two decades mourning his loss. Maeve becomes pregnant out of wedlock and works a string of odd jobs to raise her son, Jeremy. In the chaos of the German bombing of Coventry in 1940, Harriet befriends Jeremy, who, at 22, stirs intense memories of Owen. Together, they search the town for Jeremy's mother and forge an intense bond. Humphreys's characters are given to poetic tendencies that occasionally yield interesting insights on the nature of loss and change, though the cast tends toward the indistinct and the narrative feels too in service of the historical record.

Movies to see

Lady Godiva (2008)

It is a British romantic comedy film made in 2006 and released in 2008. Based on the historic tale of Lady Godiva, it was set in modern-day Oxford. Jemmima Honey, a teacher, needs to raise funds for her local creative arts centre. She accepts the challenge of riding through the streets of Oxford naked.

Shakespeare in Love (1998)

Romantic comedy set in London in the late 16th century: Young playwright William Shakespeare struggles with his latest work "Romeo and Ethel the Pirate's Daughter". A great fan of Shakespeare's plays is young, wealthy Viola who is about to be married to the cold-hearted Lord Wessex, but constantly dreams of becoming an actress. Women were not allowed to act on stage at that time (female roles were played by men, too), but dressed up as a boy, Viola successfully auditions for the part of Romeo. Soon she and William are caught in a forbidden romance that provides rich inspiration for his play.

Hamlet (1996)

It is a 1996 film version of William Shakespeare's classic play of the same name, adapted and directed by Kenneth Branagh, who also stars in the title role as Prince Hamlet. It is set in the 19th century. Hamlet, son of the king of Denmark, is summoned home for his father's funeral and his mother's wedding to his uncle. In a supernatural episode, he discovers that his uncle, whom he hates anyway, murdered his father. In an incredibly convoluted plot—the most complicated and most interesting in all literature—he manages to (impossible to put this in exact order) feign (or perhaps not to feign) madness, murder the "prime minister", love and then unlove an innocent whom he drives to madness, plot and then unplot against the uncle, direct a play within a play, successfully conspire against the lives of two well-meaning friends, and finally take his revenge on the uncle, but only at the cost of almost every life on stage, including his own and his mother's.

Songs to enjoy

Three Shakespeare Songs

It is a piece of classical choral music written for an a cappella SATB choir. It was written in 1951 by the British classical composer Ralph Vaughan Williams. The work comprises three short pieces which are settings of text from two plays by the English playwright William Shakespeare. It is published by Oxford University Press.

The text of each song is derived from plays by William Shakespeare:

Full Fathom Five
The Tempest, Act 1 scene 2
Full fathom five thy father lies,
Of his bones are coral made;
Those are pearls that were his eyes:
Nothing of him that doth fade,
But doth suffer a sea-change into something rich and strange.
Sea-nymphs hourly ring his knell:
Ding-dong.
Hark! now I hear them, ding-dong bell.

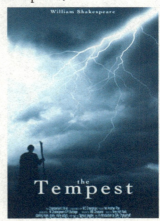

The Cloud-Capp'd Towers
The Tempest, Act IV scene 1

The cloud-capp'd towers, the gorgeous palaces,
The solemn temples, the great globe itself,
Yea, all which it inherit, shall dissolve,
And, like this insubstantial pageant faded,
Leave not a rack behind: We are such stuff
As dreams are made on, and our little life
Is rounded with a sleep.

Over Hill, Over Dale
A Midsummer Night's Dream, Act II scene 1

Over hill, over dale,
Thorough bush, thorough briar,
Over park, over pale,
Thorough flood, thorough fire
I do wander everywhere.
Swifter than the moonè's sphere;
And I serve the fairy queen,
To dew her orbs upon the green.
The cowslips tall her pensioners be;
In their gold coats spots you see;
Those be rubies, fairy favours,
In those freckles live their savours:
I must go seek some dew-drops here,
And hang a pearl in every cowslip's ear.

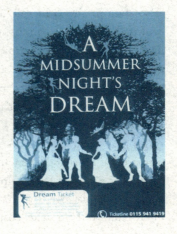

Unit 9
North West England

> Manchester's got everything except a beach.
> —Lan Brown

Unit Goals

- To have a general idea of the geography of North West England
- To be familiar with the geographical terms about North West England
- To be able to introduce North West England
- To be able to describe the Lake District, Liverpool and Manchester
- To be able to use the conjunctions properly

Before You Read

1. Do you still remember the Lake District? It is located in the county of _____ in _____ England. _____, the largest lake in England is there.
2. Do you know these two football teams? Where are they?

Cumbria
THE LAKE DISTRICT

3. Do you know any famous band in the world? Which of the following is the Beatles, and which one is the Rolling Stones? The Beatles were from _____, England.

4. **Group Work**: Form groups of three or four students. Try to find, on the Internet or in the library, more information about North West England, for example, its landscape, its famous people, one of its towns and cities, which interests you most. Get ready for a 5-minute presentation in class.

Text A View of North West England

Location and Composition

North West England is one of the nine official regions of England. It has a population of 6,853,200 and comprises five counties of England—Cumbria, Lancashire, Greater Manchester, Merseyside and Cheshire.

North West England is bounded on the west by the Irish Sea and on the east by the Pennine mountain range. The region extends from the Scottish borders in the north to the Welsh mountains in the south.

Landscape

A wide, fertile plain in the west slopes up to the Pennine Hills in the east. The northeastern part of the region, which lies to the east of the M6 motorway, is an area of wide-open spaces, including Bleasdale Moor and the Forest of Bowland. The region's main rivers are the Lune in the north, the Ribble and, in the south, the river Mersey.

Cumbria is England's second largest county, covering 6810 square kilometres (2629 miles). It is known as the Lake District because it contains 15 large lakes, the biggest of which is Windermere. The county has England's biggest mountains—Scafell Pike is the highest Peak. The area of the Cumbrian Mountains is the most rugged in England.

Important Towns and Cities

Manchester and Liverpool are the Northwest's largest cities and both are important ports. Liverpool is Britain's second largest port after London and is in the area known as Merseyside because it stands on the river Mersey. The port of Manchester lies 58 kilometers **inland** but is connected to the sea by the Manchester  Ship Canal. Both these cities are probably best known for their football teams! Liverpool is also famous as being the home of the Beatles. Their first single "Love Me Do" was **released** in October 1963. Manchester and Liverpool both have busy airports. Chester is Cheshire's chief town. Another large town is Blackpool famous for its **illuminations**.

1. Liverpool

Liverpool, with its famous waterfront on the River Mersey, is a great shipping port and industrial center. King John launched it on its road to **glory** when he **granted** it a charter in 1207. Before that, it had been a tiny 12th-century fishing village, but it quickly became a port for shipping men and materials to Ireland. In 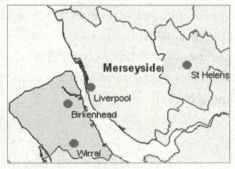 the 18th century, it grew to **prominence** because of the sugar, spice, and tobacco trade with the Americans. By the time Victoria came to the throne, Liverpool had become Britain's biggest commercial seaport.

Recent **refurbishing** of the Albert Dock, the establishment of a Maritime Museum, and the **conversion** of warehouses into little stores similar to those in San Francisco's Ghirardelli Square have made this an **up-and-coming** area once again, with many attractions for visitors. Liverpudlians are proud of their city, with its new hotels, two cathedrals, shopping and entertainment complexes, and parks. And of course, whether they're fans of the Fab Four or not, most visitors to Liverpool want to see where Beatlemania began.

2. Manchester

Manchester is a relatively new city. Born of the Industrial Revolution, it took the lead in the world's textile manufacture and production in the late 18th century, a position it held until its decline in the 1960s. Leaders of commerce, science and technology, like John Dalton and Samuel Arkwright, helped create a vibrant and thriving economy—most of the nation's wealth was created in this region during Victorian times. But it was undoubtedly textiles, and other associated trades, which dominated and created a young dynamic city, whose very symbol is the worker bee—an emblem repeated in mosaics all over the floor of the Town Hall.

Manchester is one of the largest metropolitan conurbations in the United Kingdom, justly proud of its history and heritage, its culture, enterprise and its entrepreneurial spirit. In more recent times, it has had to reconfigure its traditional manufacturing base to develop thriving new technologies. It has rebuilt itself as a leading centre of modernist architecture since the terrorist bombing of the city in 1996. This new sense of vigour and dynamism is evident in the appearance of an ever increasing number of city centre hotels, luxury apartments and self-catering accommodation. It is a tribute to its people and planners of Manchester that the city arose again out of the ashes of this atrocity, phoenix-like, to become a thoroughly modern city—a leading light of the 21st century.

Industry and Farming

North West England became famous in the 18th century for spinning and weaving, and cotton mills and factories dotted the Lancashire landscape. The industrial revolution developed round Manchester. As cotton trade grew, mill towns replaced ancient cities. Modern

Manchester's industries include clothing, banking and manufacturing.

From the medieval times Cumbria mined iron core, lead and silver. This mining and the mining for coal has mainly stopped but some steel is still made in south Cumbria. The most important industry in Cumbria is power production at the Sellafield nuclear plant.

Much of the region is rich farmland. Dairy cattle **graze** on the low plains between the Pennines and the hills of North Wales. Their milk is made into **crumbly** Cheshire or Lancashire cheese.

After You Read

Knowledge Focus

1. **Fill in the blanks according to the geographical knowledge you have learned in the text above.**
    (1) North West England comprises Cumbria, Lancashire, Merseyside, Cheshire, and _____.
    (2) North West England is bounded on the west by _____ and on the east by _____ mountain range.
    (3) North West England extends from the _____ borders in the north to the _____ mountains in the south.
    (4) North West England's main rivers are the Lune in the north, the Ribble and, in the south, _____.
    (5) _____ is England's second largest county, covering 6810 square kilometres (2629 miles). It is known as _____ because it contains 15 large lakes, the biggest of which is _____.
    (6) The area of the _____ is the most rugged in England. _____ is the highest Peak.
    (7) _____ is Britain's second largest port after London and is in the area known as _____ because it stands on the river Mersey.
    (8) The port of _____ in North West England lies 58 kilometers inland but is connected to the sea by _____.
    (9) _____ is also famous as being the home of the Beatles.
    (10) The most important industry in Cumbria is _____ production at the Sellafield nuclear plant.

2. **Write T in the brackets if the statement is true and write F if it is false.**
    (1) A wide, fertile plain in the west slopes up to the Pennine Hills in the east. ( )
    (2) Windermere has England's biggest mountains—Scafell Pike is the highest Peak. ( )
    (3) Liverpool, with its famous waterfront on the River Mersey, is a great shipping

port and industrial center. King John launched it on its road to glory when he granted it a charter in 1207. (　)

(4) By the time Victoria came to the throne, Manchester had become Britain's biggest commercial seaport. (　)

(5) It was undoubtedly textiles, and other associated trades, which dominated and created a young dynamic city, whose very symbol is the queen bee—an emblem repeated in mosaics all over the floor of the Town Hall. (　)

(6) Modern Manchester's industries include clothing, banking and manufacturing. (　)

Language Focus

1. Fill in the blanks with the proper form of the words or phrases below.

lie to	come to the throne	be famous as	be proud of
comprise	be best known for	in the appearance of	be made into

(1) It has a population of 6,853,200 and _____ five counties of England—Cumbria, Lancashire, Greater Manchester, Merseyside and Cheshire.

(2) The northeastern part of the region, which _____ the east of the M6 motorway, is an area of wide-open spaces.

(3) Both these cities _____ their football teams!

(4) Liverpool _____ being the home of the Beatles.

(5) By the time Victoria _____, Liverpool had become Britain's biggest commercial seaport.

(6) Liverpudlians _____ their city, with its new hotels, two cathedrals, shopping and entertainment complexes, and parks.

(7) This new sense of vigour and dynamism is evident _____ an ever increasing number of city centre hotels, luxury apartments and self-catering accommodation.

(8) Their milk _____ crumbly Cheshire or Lancashire cheese.

2. Fill in the blanks with the appropriate form of the words in the brackets.

(1) A wide, _____ (fertility) plain in the west slopes up to the Pennine Hills in the east.

(2) The Beatles' first single "Love Me Do" was _____ (release) in October 1963.

(3) Blackpool is famous for its _____ (illuminate).

(4) In the 18th century, it grew to _____ (prominent) because of the sugar, spice, and tobacco trade with the Americans.

(5) Recent _____ (refurbish) of the Albert Dock, the _____ (establish) of a Maritime Museum, and the _____ (convert) of warehouses into little stores similar to those in San Francisco's Ghirardelli Square have made this an up-and-coming area once again.

(6) Manchester arose again out of the ashes of _____ (atrocious).

(7) Cotton mills and factories _____ (dot) the Lancashire landscape in 18th century.

(8) Modern Manchester's industries include _____ (clothes), _____ (bank) and _____ (manufacture).

(9) Dairy cattle's milk is made into _____ (crumble) Cheshire or Lancashire cheese.

3. **Fill in the blanks with the proper prepositions and adverbs that collocate with the neighboring words.**
   (1) North West England is bounded _____ the west by the Irish Sea and _____ the east by the Pennines mountain range.
   (2) Liverpool is Britain's second largest port _____ London and is in the area known as Merseyside because it stands on the river Mersey.
   (3) The port of Manchester lies 58 kilometers inland but is connected _____ the sea by the Manchester Ship Canal.
   (4) Liverpool, _____ its famous waterfront on the River Mersey, is a great shipping port and industrial center.
   (5) In the 18th century, it grew _____ prominence because of the sugar, spice, and tobacco trade with the Americans.
   (6) Manchester is a relatively new city. Born _____ the Industrial Revolution, it took the lead in the world's textile manufacture and production in the late 18th century, a position it held _____ its decline in the 1960s.
   (7) _____ more recent times, it has had to reconfigure its traditional manufacturing base to develop thriving new technologies.
   (8) The industrial revolution developed _____ Manchester. As cotton trade grew, mill towns replaced ancient cities.

4. **Select the proper conjunctions in the brackets to fill in the blanks.**
   (1) The port of Manchester lies 58 kilometers inland _____ (however, but) is connected to the say by the Manchester Ship Canal.
   (2) _____ (Before, After) King John granted Liverpool a charter in 1207, it had been a tiny 12th-century fishing village.
   (3) _____ (When, As) cotton trade grew, mill towns replaced ancient cities.
   (4) _____ (Although, Though) not an obvious tourist highlight, Birmingham serves as a gateway to England's north.
   (5) In some places women are expected to earn money _____ (though, while) men work at home and raise their children.
   (6) He stole, not _____ (because, for) he wanted the money but because he liked stealing.
   (7) _____ (Whether, If) they're fans of the Fab Four or not, most visitors to Liverpool want to see where Beatlemania began.
   (8) It must have rained last night, _____ (because, for) the ground is wet.

Comprehensive Work

1. **Pair Work**: Discuss the following questions about the cartoon with your partner.
   (1) Where is it?
   (2) What is the man doing?
   (3) Is there anything wrong with him? Can you guess why?
   (4) What is the point of the cartoon?

2. **Group Work**: Discuss the following question in groups of three or four students. Take down what you hear from your partner and later share it with other groups.

If you have a chance to visit only one of the counties in North West England, where do you want to go? And why? Give three reasons at least.

Group member			
Destination			
Reasons	1		
	2		
	3		

3. **Solo Work**: Do you know which lake is the largest in China? Have you ever been to any great lake in China? Compare any lake you know in China with the largest lake in England. Write a composition of about 300 words.

Read More

Text B   **The Beatles**

Read the passage quickly, try to guess the meaning of the underlined words and match the words with their possible explanation.

    (1) invasion   a. occurring at the beginning
    (2) initial   b. praise vociferously

(3) trend-setter   c. a strong effect
(4) acclaim   d. capable of being seen or noticed
(5) impact   e. any entry into an area not previously occupied
(6) evident   f. someone who popularizes a new fashion

The Beatles were a pop and rock group from Liverpool, England. The band are recognized for leading the mid-1960s musical "British Invasion" into the United States. Although their initial musical style was rooted in 1950s rock and roll and homegrown skiffle, the group explored genres ranging from Tin Pan Alley to psychedelic rock. Their clothes, styles, and statements made them trend-setters, while their growing social awareness saw their influence extend into the social and cultural revolutions of the 1960s.

The Beatles are one of the most commercially successful and critically acclaimed bands in the history of popular music. In the United Kingdom, The Beatles released more than 40 different singles, albums, and EPs that reached number one. This commercial success was repeated in many other countries; their record company, EMI, estimated that by 1985 they had sold over one billion records worldwide. According to the Recording Industry Association of America, The Beatles are the best-selling musical act of all time in the United States.

In 2004, Rolling Stone magazine ranked The Beatles Number 1 on its list of 100 Greatest Artists of All Time. According to that same magazine, The Beatles' innovative music and cultural impact helped define the 1960s, and their influence on pop culture is still evident today.

Proper Nouns

Beatlemania 披头士狂
Blackpool 黑泽市
Bleasdale Moor 布利斯代尔沼泽
British Invasion 不列颠入侵
Bury 伯里
Cheshire 柴郡
Chester 切斯特
County Boroughs 自治市
EMI 百代唱片公司
EP 唱片

Ghirardelli Square 吉尔德利广场
Greater Manchester 大曼彻斯特
John Dalton 约翰·道尔顿
King John 约翰王
Lancashire 兰卡斯特郡
Liverpudlians 利物浦市民
Maritime Museum 海事博物馆
Merseyside 默西塞德郡
Oldham 奥德姆
Queen Elizabeth 伊丽莎白女王

Rochdale 罗奇代尔
Samuel Arkwright 塞缪尔·阿克莱特
San Francisco 旧金山
Scafell Pike 斯可斐峰
Stockport 斯托克波特
Tameside 泰姆塞德
the Albert Dock 艾伯特码头
the Beatles 披头士(甲壳虫)乐队
the Duchy of Lancaster 兰开斯特公爵领地
the Duke of Lancaster 兰开斯特公爵
the Fab Four 披头四(甲壳虫乐队别称)
the Forest of Bowland 博兰德森林
the House of Lancaster 兰开斯特议院
the Industrial Revolution 工业革命
the Irish Sea 爱尔兰海
the Lake District 湖泊地区
the Lune 伦河(又译:月亮河)
the Manchester Ship Canal 曼彻斯特通海运河
the Metropolitan County of Greater Manchester 大曼彻斯特都市郡
the M6 motorway M6 高速公路
the Recording Industry Association of America 美国唱片工业协会
the Ribble 里布尔河
the River Mersey 默西河
the Scottish borders 苏格兰边界
the Sellafield 塞拉菲尔德
the time Victoria/ Victorian times 维多利亚女王时代
the Town Hall 市政府
Tin Pan Alley 流行歌曲出版界
Trafford 特拉福德

For Fun

Websites to visit

http://en.wikipedia.org/wiki/North_West_England

  This is a webpage about North West England, on which you can find information on its status, politics, history, statistics, environment, education, etc.

http://en.wikipedia.org/wiki/Liverpool

  This is a webpage about the City of Liverpool, on which you can read information on its history, financial industry, local government, education, gardens, etc.

http://en.wikipedia.org/wiki/Manchester

  This is a webpage about the City of Manchester, on which you can read information on its history, financial industry, local government, education, gardens, etc.

http://www.thebeatles.com/core/home/

  This is a website about the famous band—the Beatles, on which you can read the introduction to the band and hear the music by the band.

Books to read

The Book of Liverpool: A City in Short Fiction by Maria Crossan et al.

  Spanning the last five decades of Liverpool's history, the specially commissioned pieces in this collection revel in the story of the city itself—the legendary life and culture that gave the world. The Beatles, along with the struggle and tragedy, comes with growth and change in the city's

communities. Compiled to coincide with Liverpool being named the European Capital of Culture, these stories include new works by Booker Prize-winner Barry Unsworth, Whitbred Poetry Prize-winner Roger McGough, and legendary horror writer Ramsey Campbell—all of whom provide insightful and colorful perspectives on Liverpudlian life.

The Beatles: 10 Years that Shook the World by Paul Trynka

Roll up for a magical mystery tour! From the birth of the band in 1961 to the bitter break up of 1970, this day-by-day analysis of The Beatles phenomenon examines the private and public events that revolutionized the music world. From their iconic domination of the music industry to the dramatic split, rare and only recently published photographs reveal the band as never before. Written by the world's greatest rock writers Nick Kent and Raymond Jones, with contributions from key personalities of the era, including Astrid Kirchherr, Marianne Faithfull and Donovan, get the inside scoop on The Beatles and see them as you never have before. It is published in association with "Mojo" magazine.

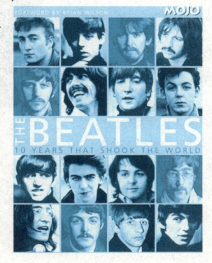

Movies to see

The 51st State (2001)

Elmo McElroy is a streetwise American master chemist who heads to England to sell his special new formula—a powerful, blue concoction guaranteed to take you to "the 51st state." McElroy's new product delivers a feeling 51 times more powerful than any thrill, any pleasure, any high in history. But his plans for a quick, profitable score go comically awry when he gets stuck in Liverpool with an unlikely escort and his ex-girlfriend and becomes entangled in a bizarre web of double-dealing and double-crosses.

A Hard Day's Night (1964)

It is a 1964 British comedy film written by Alun Owen starring The Beatles—John Lennon, Paul McCartney, George Harrison and Ringo Starr—during the height of their popularity. It was directed by Richard Lester and originally released by United Artists. The film was made in the style of a mock documentary, describing a couple of days in the lives of the group.

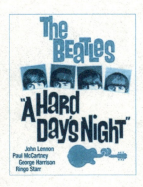

Song to enjoy

Love Me Do

Love, love me do.
You know I love you,
I'll always be true,
So please, love me do.
Whoa, love me do.
Love, love me do.
You know I love you,
I'll always be true,
So please, love me do.
Whoa, love me do.
Someone to love,
Somebody new.
Someone to love,

Someone like you.
Love, love me do.
You know I love you,
I'll always be true,
So please, love me do.
Whoa, love me do.
Love, love me do.
You know I love you,
I'll always be true,
So please, love me do.
Whoa, love me do.
Yeah, love me do.
Whoa, oh, love me do.

Unit 10

Yorkshire and the Humber

> The history of York is the history of England.
> —George VI

Unit Goals

- To have a general idea of the geography of Yorkshire and the Humber
- To be familiar with the geographical terms about Yorkshire and the Humber
- To be able to introduce Yorkshire and the Humber
- To be able to describe York and Leeds
- To be able to make comparisons in different ways

Before You Read

1. Do you still remember the spiritual capital of England? Yes, it is _____ in Kent. And _____ in Yorkshire is an ecclesiastical center equaled only by it, because of its _____ Minster.

2. In the late eighteenth and nineteenth century, _____ in Yorkshire was known as the woolen centre of the world.

3. Have you ever read the famous works—*Jane Eyre*, *Wuthering Heights* and *Agnes Grey*? They were written respectively by the Brontë sisters—_____ Brontë, _____ Brontë, and _____ Brontë.

4. If you want to go shopping in the North of England, _____ in Yorkshire, with its impressive Victorian shopping arcades, must be your destination.

5. **Group Work:** Form groups of three or four students. Try to find, on the Internet or in the library, more information about Yorkshire and the Humber, for example, one of its famous people, or one of its towns and cities, which interests you most. Get ready for a 5-minute presentation in class.

Start to Read

Text A View of Yorkshire and the Humber

Location and Composition

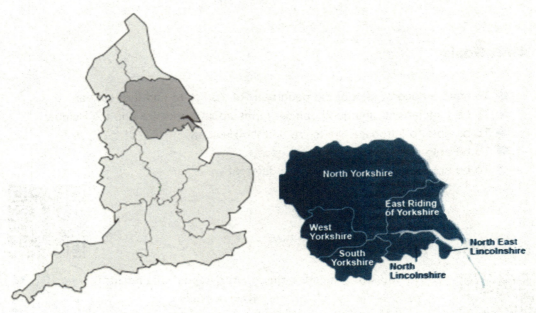

Yorkshire and the Humber is one of the nine official regions of England. It covers most of the historic county of Yorkshire, along with the part of northern Lincolnshire that was, from 1974 to 1996, within the former shire county of Humberside. The Yorkshire and the Humber region includes North Yorkshire (county), West Yorkshire (ceremonial county), South Yorkshire (ceremonial county), East Riding of Yorkshire (ceremonial county), North Lincolnshire (UA), and North East Lincolnshire (UA).

Landscape

The landscape of Yorkshire and the Humber is very varied. In the west are the Pennines and their foothills, which are divided by the Yorkshire Dales, long valleys that run from east to west. The highest Pennine peak in Yorkshire is Cross Fell (790 metres). Fast-flowing streams pass through the Dales and join the river Humber. The area **boasts** spectacular waterfalls and a **scenic** limestone landscape around Malham.

In the east, the rolling hills of the moors are covered with heather. As well as thriving towns and cities, it has more National Park land, i.e. Yorkshire Dales and the North York Moors, historic houses and castles than any other region.

There is no better place to have a canter than Yorkshire, be it alongside the Heritage Coastline, through one of the National Parks or along the bridle paths and routes specifically **intended for** the rider. This is proved by the proverb: Oxford for learning, London for wit, Hull for women and York for horses.

Important Towns and Cities

There are many famous towns and cities in Yorkshire and the Humber, such as Sheffield, Rotherham, Barnsley, Doncaster, Wakefield, Bradford, Leeds, Scarborough, York, Halifax, and Hull.

1. York

Few cities in England are as rich in history as York. It is still **encircled** by its 13th- and 14th-century city walls, about 4 km (2.49 miles) long, with four gates. One of these, Micklegate, once **grimly** greeted visitors coming from the south with the heads of **traitors**. To this day, you can walk on the footpath of the medieval walls.

The **crowning** achievement of York is its Minster, or Cathedral, which makes the city an **ecclesiastical** center equaled only by Canterbury. It is easily **visible** on a drive up to Edinburgh in Scotland.

There was a Roman York (Hadrian came this way), then a Saxon York, a Danish York, a Norman York (William the Conqueror slept here), a medieval York, a Georgian York, and a Victorian York (the center of a flourishing rail business). A large amount of 18th-century York remains for visitors to explore today, including Richard Boyle's restored Assembly Rooms.

You may want to visit the Shambles. Once

the meat-butchering center of York, it dates from before the Norman Conquest. The messy business is gone now, but the ancient street survives, filled today with jewelry stores, cafes, and buildings that huddle so closely together that you can practically stand in the middle of the pavement, arms outstretched, and touch the houses on both sides of the street.

2. Leeds

The city was originally an agricultural market town in the Middle Ages, and received its first charter in 1207. In the Tudor period, Leeds was mainly a merchant town manufacturing woolen cloths and trading with Europe via the Humber estuary. At one point, nearly half of England's total export passed through Leeds. The city's industrial growth was catalyzed by the introduction of the Leeds and Liverpool Canal in 1816 and the railway in 1848.

The vast range of attractions, thriving club scene, and world class sports and leisure venues make Leeds a brilliant place to live or visit. The city is alive with vibrant, European-style cafes sitting comfortably alongside traditional English pubs.

Leeds is also the destination for shopping in the north, with its impressive Victorian shopping arcades, and all the major high street names. Leeds plays host to the largest department store in Yorkshire, and the first Harvey Nichols outside London. Leeds is particularly good for shopping as the centre is predominantly a pedestrian-only area.

The range of restaurants is superb, with Indian, Chinese, Thai, Spanish, French, American, Italian and Mexican to choose from, in addition to the traditional English food served both in the City Centre and the quaint country pubs on the way to the Yorkshire Dales.

Industry and Farming

Engineering and textiles are the region's two top industries, and are concentrated in West and South Yorkshire. Sheffield's silver and steel industries have a worldwide name. For many years Yorkshire's coalfields provided much of the fuel used in British industry, but most mines have now closed.

Dairy farmers in the Dales make delicious cheeses such as Wensleydale and Swaledale. The moors provide rough grazing for sheep.

After You Read

Knowledge Focus

1. **Fill in the blanks according to the geographical knowledge you have learned in the text above.**
   (1) Yorkshire and the Humber covers most of the historic county of _____, along with the part of northern _____ that was, from 1974 to 1996, within the former shire county of Humberside.
   (2) In the west of Yorkshire and the Humber are _____ and their foothills, which are divided by _____, long valleys that run from east to west.
   (3) There are two national parks in Yorkshire and the Humber; one is Yorkshire Dales, the other _____.
   (4) _____, a unitary authority with a long history, is located in North Yorkshire.

2. **Write T in the brackets if the statement is true and write F if it is false.**
   (1) Yorkshire and the Humber is one of the eight official regions of England. (　)
   (2) The landscape of Yorkshire and the Humber is very varied. (　)
   (3) Many cities in England are as rich in history as York. (　)
   (4) Shambles was once the meat-butchering center of York. (　)
   (5) Leeds was originally an agricultural market town in the Middle Ages. (　)
   (6) At one point, nearly all of England's total export passed through Leeds. (　)

Language Focus

1. **Fill in the blanks with the proper form of the words or phrases below.**

be gone	be concentrated in	remain
play host to	so...that...	

   (1) Engineering and textiles are the region's two top industries, and _____ West and South Yorkshire.
   (2) A large amount of 18th-century York _____ for visitors to explore today, including Richard Boyle's restored Assembly Rooms.
   (3) The buildings on that street huddle _____ closely together _____ you can practically stand in the middle of the pavement, arms outstretched, and touch the houses on both sides of the street.
   (4) The messy business _____ now, but the ancient street survives.
   (5) Leeds _____ the largest department store in Yorkshire, and the first Harvey Nichols outside London.

2. **Fill in the blanks with the appropriate form of the words in the brackets.**
   (1) York is still _____ (circle) by its 13th- and 14th-century city walls, about 4 km (2.49 miles) long, with four gates.
   (2) The crowning achievement of York is its minster, or cathedral, which makes the

city an _____ (ecclesiastically) center equaled only by Canterbury.
(3) The Cathedral in York is easily _____ (visibility) on a drive up to Edinburgh in Scotland.
(4) The _____ (mess) business is gone now, but the ancient street _____ (survival), filled today with jewelry stores, cafes, and building.
(5) Industrial growth of Leeds was _____ (catalysis) by the introduction of the Leeds and Liverpool Canal in 1816 and the railway in 1848.
(6) Leeds is particularly good for shopping as the centre is _____ (predominant) a _____ (pedestrianism)-only area.
(7) The range of restaurants is _____ (superbness), with _____ (India), Chinese, _____ (Thailand), _____ (Spain), French, American, Italian and _____ (Mexico) to choose from, in addition to the traditional English food.

3. **Fill in the blanks with the proper prepositions and adverbs that collocate with the neighboring words.**
(1) The village was founded sometime _____ the time of the Norman Conquest.
(2) The moors provide rough grazing _____ sheep.
(3) In the Tudor period Leeds was mainly a merchant town manufacturing woolen cloths and trading with Europe _____ the Humber estuary.
(4) The city is alive with vibrant, European-style cafes sitting comfortably _____ traditional English pubs.
(5) The area boasts spectacular waterfalls and a scenic limestone landscape _____ Malham.
(6) Leeds is the destination _____ shopping in the north, with its impressive Victorian shopping arcades, and all the major high street names.
(7) Fast-flowing streams pass _____ the Dales and join the river Humber.

4. **Translate the following sentences into Chinese. Pay attention to how comparison is made.**
(1) There is no better place to have a canter than Yorkshire.
(2) Few cities in England are as rich in history as York.
(3) The dining-room is twice as big as the kitchen.
(4) She is as good a cook as her mother.
(5) He is more than a father to her.
(6) They were more than glad to help.
(7) He is said to pay less income tax than he should.
(8) A half truth is often no better than a lie.

Comprehensive Work
1. **Solo Work:** Please locate the following places on the map:
North Yorkshire
West Yorkshire
South Yorkshire

East Riding of Yorkshire
North Lincolnshire
North East Lincolnshire
York
Leeds
Bradford

2. **Pair Work**: Discuss the following questions about the cartoon with your partner.
   (1) Who are they?
   (2) Where are they?
   (3) What are they doing?
   (4) What does the woman mean by saying "To Eyre is human!"?
   (5) Have you ever heard of "To err is human."? What does it mean? And do you agree?

"So what if I read gothies all the time? To Eyre is human!"

3. **Solo Work**: Suppose you are a clerk in some travel agency in the North West of England. Write a passage, introducing a traveling route to Yorkshire and the Humber, which should include the time, the fee, the cities to visit, the things to do, the hotels to stay, and the food to eat, etc. Try to make it as fascinating as possible within the limit of 300 words.

Read More

Text B   Bradford

Read the passage quickly and try to find the answer to the following questions.
1. Where is Bradford located?
2. What was it famous for? How about now?

Bradford is an industrial city on the edge of the moors of the Britain's West Yorkshire Pennines and in the heart of Brontë Country—where the Brontë sisters were born and lived and wrote their classic novels.

Founded sometime around the time of the Norman Conquest, the original village of Bradford **sprang up** around the "Broad Ford" crossing Bradford Beck at church bank, by the site of Bradford Cathedral on the edge of what is now known as Little Germany. However, it was not until the industrial revolution, in the late eighteenth and nineteenth century that Bradford grew and gained importance as a major producer of textiles and became known as the woolen centre of the world.

To support the textiles mills and machinery, a large manufacturing base grew up in the city, leading to **diversification** with different industries thriving side by side. Today most of the older textile mills and some of the heavier industries have closed, but Bradford remains one of the north's important cities, with modern engineering, chemicals, digital media, I.T. and financial services (especially building societies) replacing the "dark **satanic** mills" of the industrial revolution.

Bradford Industrial Museum

Despite its industrial past, the city of Bradford is situated near to the very edge of the West Yorkshire conurbation, with the wide open spaces of Baildon Moor and Rombalds Moor lying very close by, the wild Pennine moors of Haworth and the heart of Brontë Country lying immediately to the west, and the stunningly beautiful Yorkshire Dales beginning only about fifteen miles away to the approximate north west.

Proper Nouns

Agnes Grey 《艾格尼丝·格雷》
Assembly Rooms 宴会厅(又译:集会厅)
Baildon Moor 贝尔顿沼泽
Barnsley 班士利
Bradford 布拉德福德
Bradford Cathedral 布拉德福德大教堂
Brontë Country 勃朗特地区
Castle Howard 霍华德城堡(霍华堡)
Cross Fell 克罗斯费尔峰
Danish 丹麦的
Doncaster 唐卡斯特
Georgian 乔治王时代
Hadrian 哈德良(罗马帝王)

Halifax 哈利法克斯
Harvey Nichols 哈威·尼古拉斯百货公司
Haworth 哈沃斯
Hull 赫尔
Humberside 亨伯赛德郡
Jane Eyre 《简·爱》
Leeds 利兹
Lincolnshire 林肯郡
Liverpool Canal 利物浦运河
Malham 马勒姆村
North York Moors 北约克郡荒原/高沼/湿地国家公园
Richard Boyle 理查德·波意耳

Rombalds Moor 罗姆伯尔德沼泽
Rotherham 罗瑟汉姆
Saxon 撒克逊人的
Scarborough 斯卡布罗
Sheffield 谢菲尔德
Swaledale 斯韦尔代尔奶酪
the Humber 亨伯河
the Norman Conquest 诺曼征服
the Shambles 肉市场
the Tudor period 都铎王朝
Victorian 维多利亚时期
Wakefield 韦可菲尔德
Wensleydale 文斯勒代尔奶酪
Wuthering Heights《呼啸山庄》
York 约克
Yorkshire 约克郡
Yorkshire Dales 约克郡溪谷国家公园

For Fun

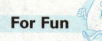

Websites to visit

http://en.wikipedia.org/wiki/Yorkshire

　　This is a webpage about Yorkshire, on which you can find information on its history, geography, economy, transport, culture, governance, etc.

http://en.wikipedia.org/wiki/Bront%C3%AB

　　This is a webpage about the Brontë sisters, on which you can find information on the three sisters, their influence and their works.

Books to read

Jane Eyre by Charlotte Brontë

　　Jane Eyre ranks as one of the greatest and most perennially popular works of English fiction. Although the poor but plucky heroine is outwardly of plain appearance, she possesses an indomitable spirit, a sharp wit and great courage. She is forced to battle against the exigencies of a cruel guardian, a harsh employer and a rigid social order, all of which circumscribe her life and position when she becomes governess to the daughter of the mysterious, sardonic and attractive Mr. Rochester.

　　However, there is great kindness and warmth in this epic love story, which is set against the magnificent backdrop of the Yorkshire moors.

Wuthering Heights by Emily Brontë

　　It is Emily Brontë's only novel. It was first published in 1847 under the pseudonym Ellis Bell, and a posthumous second edition was edited by her sister Charlotte. The name of the novel comes from the Yorkshire manor on the moors on which the story centres. (As an adjective, wuthering is a Yorkshire word referring to turbulent weather.) The narrative tells the tale of

the all-encompassing and passionate, yet thwarted love between Heathcliff and Catherine Earnshaw, and how this unresolved passion eventually destroys both themselves and many around them.

Movies to see

Jane Eyre (1996)

Jane Eyre, orphaned, is left to live under the charity of her Aunt Reed. After living ten years of mistreatment and segregation in her Aunt's home, she is then sent to Lowood—a boarding school for young girls. Jane grows up both physically and mentally at Lowood and becomes a teacher at age eighteen. She then advertises for the position of a governess and is called upon by Mrs Fairfax at Thornfield. At Thornfield, Jane falls in love with the master, Mr Rochester, and he with her. However, he yields a terrible and dark secret that threatens to tear them apart for good.

Wuthering Heights (1992)

Heathcliff is Cathy Earnshaw's foster brother; more than that, he is her other half. When forces tear them apart, Heathcliff wreaks vengeance on those he holds responsible, even into a second generation.

Brontë (2008)

On the wet and wuthering moors of 19th century Yorkshire, the Brontë sisters emerge from the haven of their hidden fantasy worlds, from beneath the wing of their eccentric, domineering father and their beloved brother's drug-addled demise, to become history's most famous authors.

Song to enjoy

Leeds! Leeds! Leeds!
by Les Reed and Barry Mason

Leeds! Leeds! Leeds!, commonly known as *Marching On Together*, is the name of the anthem of Leeds United A.F.C. The song is played just before kick-off at every home game at Elland Road and it is a ritual for every Leeds United fan to stand up and sing when it is played.

**LEEDS, LEEDS, LEEDS
(Marching On Together)**

Here we go with Leeds United
We're gonna give the boys a hand
Stand up and sing for Leeds United
They are the greatest in the land

Every day, we're all gonna say
We love you Leeds—Leeds—Leeds
Everywhere, we're gonna be there
We love you Leeds—Leeds—Leeds
Marching on together
We're gonna see you win (na, na, na, na, na, na)
We are so proud
We shout it out loud
We love you Leeds—Leeds—Leeds

We've been through it all together
And we've had our up's and down's

We're gonna stay with you forever
At least until the world stops going 'round

Every day, we're all gonna say
We love you Leeds—Leeds—Leeds
Everywhere, we're gonna be there
We love you Leeds—Leeds—Leeds
Marching on together
We're gonna see you win (na, na, na, na, na, na)
We are so proud
We shout it out loud
We love you Leeds—Leeds—Leeds

We are so proud
We shout it out loud
We love you Leeds—Leeds—Leeds

Unit 11
North East England

> Newcastle appealed to us for many different reasons.
> —Mike Jefferies

Unit Goals

- To have a general idea of the geography of North East England
- To be familiar with the geographical terms about North East England
- To be able to introduce North East England
- To be able to describe the Hadrian's Wall ard Newcastle
- To be able to compare and contrast North East and South West
- To be able to use the emphatic pattern more flexibly

 ### Before You Read

1. Have you visited the Great Wall in China? How about the "Great Wall" in England? It is _____ Wall? Where is it? Who built it? And for what?

2. Situated on the north bank of the River Tyne, _____ is linked to _____ by a series of seven bridges and the two centers form an exciting destination that is positively buzzing with creativity and energy.

3. The painting on the right is by the famous painter—L. S. Lowry about _____, a city in

the north Northumberland.
4. What is the largest forested area in England and where is it?
5. **Group Work**: Form groups of three or four students. Try to find, on the Internet or in the library, more information about North East England, for example, its landscape, or one of its towns and cities, which interests you most. Get ready for a 5-minute presentation in class.

Start to Read

Text A View of North East England

Location and Composition

North East England, one of the nine official regions of England, is located in the North East of England and comprises the combined area of Northumberland, County Durham, Tyne and Wear and Teesside.

Landscape

As well as its urban centres of Tyneside, Wearside and Teesside, North East England is also noted for the richness of its natural beauty. Northumberland National Park, the region's coastline, its section of the Pennines and Weardale provide evidence for this. It also has great historic importance, the evidence of which is seen in Northumberland's Castles and the two World

Heritage Sites of Durham Cathedral and Hadrian's Wall. The highest point in the region is the Cheviot, in Northumberland, at 815 metres (2,674 ft).

Important Towns and Cities

Newcastle-upon-Tyne is the biggest city; others include historic Berwick-upon-Tweed, Sunderland and the cathedral city of Durham. Important towns include Tynemouth, Gateshead and Stockton-on-Tees.

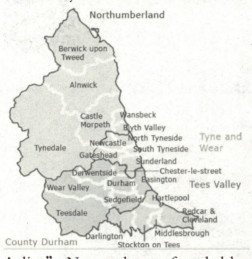

1. Newcastle-upon-Tyne

Situated on the north bank of the River Tyne, Newcastle is linked to Gateshead by a series of seven bridges and the two centers form an exciting destination that is **positively buzzing** with **creativity** and energy.

Far more than just another northern conurbation, NewcastleGateshead is vibrant and energetic with a rich history that seems to be **etched** onto every street corner. Originally known as "Pons Aelius", Newcastle was founded by the Roman emperor Hadrian between 120 A.D. and 128 A.D., and a **sizeable** section of his wall is still visible close to the city today. After the Romans came the Normans, and in 1080 Robert Curthose, son of William the Conqueror, built the wooden "Novum Castellum" or New Castle, from which the city takes its name. Coal exportation became the mainstay of the economy which **paved the way for** the development of shipbuilding and other successful heavy industries. But these fell into decline in the latter half of the 20th century and the city was forced to **reinvent** itself.

It was through art that NewcastleGateshead **spearheaded** an incredible period of **regeneration**, and art is very much a part of the area's modern identity. The region reborn, it has regained its confident **swagger** to become the crowning jewel of the North East.

2. Berwick-upon-Tweed

Berwick-upon-Tweed is situated in north Northumberland on the border with Scotland. The town is a true gem and boasts amazing architecture that still holds **fascinating** clues to centuries of its **turbulent** history, all in the most unspoilt and beautiful of settings. The most famous architectural icon is the Town Wall that still encircles over 260 listed buildings and graceful Georgian architecture. It is the only intact Elizabethan Town Wall remaining in England. When it was built in 1558, it was and still is the most expensive undertaking of England's Golden Age!

The most eye catching construction are three bridges over the wide estuary of the river Tweed, built in 1634, 1928 and 1850. The latter was designed by Robert Stephenson and is being hailed as one of the finest railway viaducts in the world. A most awe-inspiring view is still glimpsed from the train when it crosses over this bridge, with a view over Berwick nestled on the banks of the River Tweed and down the length of the coast with Bamburgh Castle and Lindisfarne in the background.

Walking the Elizabethan fortifications is a great way to appreciate Berwick's history and to take in the stunning views over the town and the wide sandy beaches of the North Sea and the Tweed estuary with its colony of mute swans. However, Berwick's charm today belies its turbulent past, as the town was captured or sacked 13 times before 1482 when it became English.

Berwick's beauty did not remain unnoticed and one of the more famous frequent visitors was L. S. Lowry. There is a "Lowry Trail" for those who want to explore this famous painter's favorite holiday resort.

Today the town is home to a thriving arts and culture scene with some great museums and galleries, as well as unique events such as the Riding of the Bounds and Border Marches, celebrating the unique town boundaries.

Industry

From the medieval times, Northumberland mined iron core, lead and silver. This mining and the mining for coal has stopped. Northumberland's shipbuilding and glass-making have also declined. Now the county produces electrical machinery and pottery. There are manufacturing and engineering industries in parts of Durham and Tyne and Wear. Tyneside was once the country's chief producer of salt, which was extracted from the North Sea.

Farming, Fishing and Forestry

Sheep farming is the main agricultural activity in this bleak and rugged region. The rivers Eden, Derwent, Tyne and Tweed are all important salmon fisheries. The Kielder forest, the largest forested area in England, is a major timber producer.

After You Read

Knowledge Focus

1. **Fill in the blanks according to the geographical knowledge you have learned in the text above.**

   (1) North East England comprises the combined area of _____, County Durham, Tyne and Wear and Teesside.

   (2) _____ National Park is in North East England.

   (3) North East England has two World Heritage Sites. They are Durham Cathedral and _____.

   (4) _____ was founded by the Roman emperor _____ between AD 120 and 128, and a sizeable section of his wall is still visible close to the city today. After the Romans came the Normans, and in 1080 Robert Curthose, son of _____, built the wooden "Novum Castellum", from which the city takes its name.

   (5) _____ is the most northerly town in Northumberland, lying on the Scottish border.

   (6) _____ is the largest forested area in England.

2. **Write T in the brackets if the statement is true and write F if it is false.**

   (1) Situated on the north bank of the River Tyne, Newcastle is linked to Gateshead by a series of six bridges and the two centers form an exciting destination that is positively buzzing with creativity and energy. ( )

   (2) It was through industry that NewcastleGateshead spearheaded an incredible period of regeneration. ( )

   (3) The most famous architectural icon is the Town Wall that still encircles over 260 listed buildings and graceful Georgian architecture. ( )

   (4) From the medieval times, Northumberland mined iron core, gold and silver. ( )

(5) Tyneside was once the country's chief producer of salt, which was extracted from the North Sea. (　)
(6) Sheep farming is the main agricultural activity in North East England. (　)

Language Focus

1. **Fill in the blanks with the proper form of the phrases below.**

be extracted from	pave the way for	be noted for
be hailed as	provide...for	take one's name
be linked to	take in	

   (1) As well as its urban centres of Tyneside, Wearside and Teesside, North East England _____ the richness of its natural beauty.
   (2) Situated on the north bank of the River Tyne, Newcastle _____ Gateshead by a series of seven bridges and the two centers.
   (3) After the Romans came the Normans, and in 1080 Robert Curthose, son of William the Conqueror, built the wooden "Novum Castellum" or New Castle, from which the city _____.
   (4) Walking the Elizabethan fortifications is a great way to appreciate Berwick's history and to _____ the views over the town.
   (5) Tyneside was once the country's chief producer of salt, which _____ the North Sea.
   (6) Northumberland National Park, the region's coastline, its section of the Pennines and Weardale _____ evidence _____ this.
   (7) The latter was designed by Robert Stephenson and _____ one of the finest railway viaducts in the world.
   (8) Coal exportation became the mainstay of the economy which _____ the development of shipbuilding and other successful heavy industries.

2. **Fill in the blanks with the appropriate form of the words in the brackets.**

   (1) North East England is noted for the _____ (rich) of its natural beauty.
   (2) Coal _____ (export) became the mainstay of the _____ (economical) which _____ (pavement) the way for the development of shipbuilding and other successful heavy industries.
   (3) Through art, NewcastleGateshead spearheaded an _____ (incredibility) period of _____ (regenerate), and art is very much a part of the area's modern identity.
   (4) The region reborn, it has regained its _____ (confidence) swagger to become the _____ (crown) jewel of the North East.
   (5) The two centers form an exciting destination that is _____ (positive) buzzing with _____ (creative) and _____ (energetic).
   (6) Berwick-upon-Tweed is a true gem and boasts _____ (amaze) architecture that still holds _____ (fascinate) clues to centuries of its _____ (turbulence) history.

(7) The most eye _____ (catch) construction are three bridges over the wide estuary of the river Tweed, built in 1634, 1928 and 1850.

(8) Walking the Elizabethan _____ (fortify) is a great way to appreciate Berwick's history and to take in the _____ (stun) views over the town and the wide _____ (sand) beaches of the North Sea and the Tweed estuary with its colony of _____ (muteness) swans.

(9) The town is home to a _____ (thrive) arts and culture scene.

(10) Tyneside was once the country's chief _____ (produce) of salt, which was _____ (extraction) from the North Sea.

3. **Fill in the blanks with the proper prepositions and adverbs that collocate with the neighboring words.**

(1) Far more than just another northern conurbation, NewcastleGateshead is vibrant and energetic _____ a rich history that seems to be etched _____ every street corner.

(2) The town is a true gem and boasts amazing architecture that still holds fascinating clues _____ centuries of its turbulent history, all _____ the most unspoilt and beautiful of settings.

(3) The most famous architectural icon is the Town Wall that still encircles _____ 260 listed buildings and graceful Georgian architecture.

(4) A most awe-inspiring view is still glimpsed _____ the train when it crosses _____ this bridge, with a view over Berwick nestled on the banks of the River Tweed and _____ the length of the coast _____ Bamburgh Castle and Lindisfarne in the background.

(5) There is a "Lowry Trail" _____ those who want to explore this famous painter's favorite holiday resort.

(6) Today the town is home _____ a thriving arts and culture scene with some great museums and galleries.

(7) There are manufacturing and engineering industries _____ parts of Durham and Tyne and Wear.

4. **Rewrite the following sentences in the emphatic pattern (it is/was... that...), by emphasizing the words in bold.**

(1) NewcastleGateshead spearheaded an incredible period of regeneration through art.

(2) You can see this kind of flower in May.

(3) Lack of money, not of effort, defeated their plan.

(4) Not who is right but what is right is of importance.

(5) Did Jim tell us the new?

(6) I just wonder what makes him so excited.

(7) I didn't realize she was a famous film star until she took off her dark glasses.

(8) Our being late caused him to serve dinner an hour later than usual.

Comprehensive Work

1. **Group Work**: Here is an England's National Parks Map. Do you still remember their names? Do you remember their distinct features? Discuss them in groups of three or four students.

2. **Pair Work**: Discuss the following questions about the cartoon with your partner.

   (1) Who are they in the Cartoon?

   (2) What are they doing?

   (3) What does the sentence "You're putting up too many walls Hadrian." imply?

3. **Solo Work**: Compare the North East with the South West in terms of location, rivers, national parks, World Heritage Sites, and cities. Write a composition within 300 words.

"You're putting up too many walls hadrian."

Read More

Text B   **Hadrian's Wall**

Read the passage quickly and find the answer to the following questions.

1. When and where was Hadrian's Wall built?

2. How tall and wide is it?
3. What was it built for?
4. Who built it?

Hadrian's Wall was built on the orders of the Emperor Hadrian. The **primary** function of Hadrian's Wall was to keep out the Picts. The Roman Army had advanced into north England but attacks by the Picts made life difficult for them. Hadrian's Wall was started in A. D. 122 and it remains a **remarkable** piece of engineering in the environment it was built in.

Hadrian's Wall is 117 kilometers long and is built in stone. In places it is six meters high and three meters wide—enough for two soldiers to do sentry duty side-by-side. Every Roman mile (about 1500 meters) a mile-castle was built which housed twenty soldiers. Turrets guarded by soldiers were built

every 500 meters. Major forts such as the one at Housesteads, were built along the wall at every eight kilometers. These could **accommodate** between 500 and 1000 Roman soldiers. Housesteads had a hospital, granary, barracks, workshop and washroom/toilets built. Stored grain was kept dry by the use of a hypocaust—this way, soldiers always had a reasonable supply of food. A Roman road called the Stanegate was built to supply the soldiers based at Hadrian's Wall.

All the building was done by the Roman soldiers themselves. They were trained to do this and the army had its own skilled engineers who designed the wall. That so much of the Wall has survived is a **testament** to their building skills.

The Picts nearly destroyed the wall three times but on every occasion it was rebuilt by the Romans. For nearly 250 years, Hadrian's Wall was **patrolled** and guarded—right on the very edge of the Roman Empire.

Proper Nouns

Bamburgh Castle 班博城堡
Berwick 贝利克郡
Berwick-upon-Tweed 特威德河畔贝利克

County Durham 达勒姆郡
Derwent 德文特河
Durham 达勒姆

Unit 11　North East England

Durham Castle 达勒姆城堡
Durham Dales 达勒姆河谷
Elizabethan Town Wall 伊丽莎白时代的城墙
England's Golden Age 英格兰的黄金时代
Gateshead 盖茨谢德
Georgian architecture 佐治亚王时代的建筑
Hadrian's Wall 哈德良长城
Housesteads 豪斯戴德
Lindisfarne 林迪斯法恩
L. S. Lowry 劳伦斯·斯蒂文·洛利
Newcastle 纽卡斯尔
NewcastleGateshead 纽卡斯尔盖茨海德
Newcastle-upon-Tyne 泰恩河畔纽卡斯尔
Northumberland 诺森伯兰郡
Northumberland's Castles 诺森伯兰郡城堡
Northumberland National Park 诺森伯兰郡国家公园
Novum Castellum (拉丁语) 纽卡斯尔
Pons Aelius 庞斯艾利乌斯
Robert Curthose 罗贝尔二世(外号柯索斯)
Robert Stephenson 罗伯特·史蒂文森
St. Cuthbert 圣卡丝柏
Stockton-on-Tees 蒂斯河畔斯托克

Sunderland 桑德兰
Teesside 蒂斯河畔
the Cheviot 切维厄特
the Elizabethan fortifications 伊丽莎白时代的要塞
the Emperor Hadrian 哈德良大帝
the Kielder forest 开尔德森林
the Normans 诺曼人
the North Pennines 北奔宁山脉
the Picts 皮克特人
the Rivers Eden 伊甸园之河
The River Tees 蒂斯河
the River Tweed 翠儿河
the River Tyne 泰恩河
the River Wear 威尔河
the Romans 罗马人
the Roman Army 罗马军队
Tyne and Wear 泰恩-威尔
Tynemouth 泰恩茅斯
Tyneside 泰恩河畔
Wear 威尔河
Weardale 威尔代尔河谷
Wearside 威尔河畔

For Fun

Websites to visit

http://en.wikipedia.org/wiki/North_East_England

　　This is a webpage about North East England, on which you can find information on its status, politics, history, statistics, environment, education, etc.

http://en.wikipedia.org/wiki/Newcastle-upon-Tyne

　　This is a webpage about Newcastle-upon-Tyne, on which you can read information on its history, financial industry, local government, education, gardens, etc.

http://en.wikipedia.org/wiki/Berwick-upon-Tweed

　　This is a webpage about the famous buildings and landmarks, governance, economy, transport, culture and the like of Berwick-upon-Tweed.

http://en.wikipedia.org/wiki/Hadrian%E2%80%99s_wall

　　This is a website of Hadrian's Wall, on which you can find a lot of interesting information about it.

英国国情 英国自然人文地理(第2版)

Book to read

The Millennium History of North East England by David Simpson

The last ten years of the second millennium saw the closure of County Durham's last coal mine, ending an era of at least 800 years. A huge football stadium was built in its place, one of many modern developments in the 1990s. The developments were to rejuvenate the region and its economy and most of them were concentrated in the old riverside areas of the Tyne, Wear and Tees which had once been at the forefront of the old manufacturing economy. Today the major industries which dominated the North-East throughout the 19th and 20th centuries have declined or disappeared, leaving the region to adjust to new technologies, new forms of employment and a new way of life.

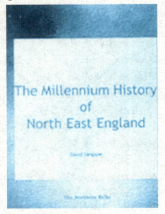

Movie to see

Wetherby (1985)

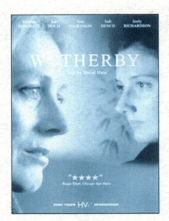

Set in the town of Wetherby in West Yorkshire, the film focuses on Jean Travers, a middle-aged spinster schoolteacher. One evening, she invites married friends for a dinner party, only to have some terrible repressions and past traumas dredged up when guest John Morgan expresses his emotional pain. The strange young man arrives at Jean's cottage the next morning with a gift of pheasants. While sitting at the kitchen table waiting for tea, he inexplicably and without warning puts the barrel of a gun in his mouth and kills himself.

Song to enjoy

Fare Thee Well Northumberland by Mark Knopfler

Come drive me down to the central station
I hate to leave my river Tyne
For some damn town that's God-forsaken
Fare thee well, Northumberland
Although I'll go where the lady takes me
She'll never tell what's in her hand
I do not know what fate awaits me
Fare thee well, Northumberland

My heart beats for my streets and alley
Longs to Dwell in the borderlands
The North-East shore and the river valleys
Fare thee well Northumberland
I may not stay, I'm bound for leaving
I'm bound to ramble and to roam
I only say my heart is grieving
I would not gamble on my coming home

Roll on, Geordie boy, roll
Roll on, Geordie boy, roll
Roll on, Geordie boy, roll
Roll on, Geordie boy, roll

So drive me down to the central station
I hate to leave my river Tyne
For some damn town that's God-forsaken
Goodbye old friend of mine
Although I'll go where the lady takes me
She'll never tell what's in her hand
I do not know what fate awaits me
Fare thee well, Northumberland

So roll on, Geordie boy, roll
Roll on, Geordie boy, roll
Roll on, Geordie boy, roll
Roll on, Geordie boy, roll

Unit 12
Scotland

> We look to Scotland for all our ideas of civilization
> —Voltaire

Unit Goals

- To have a general idea of the geography of Scotland
- To be familiar with the geographical terms about Scotland
- To be able to introduce Scotland
- To be able to describe Lock Ness, Edinbourgh and Glasgow
- To be able to compare and contrast England and Scotland
- To be able to use attributive nouns more skillfully

Before You Read

1. Do you know the following local specialties of Scotland? Can you match them with their names?

(　　)　　　(　　)　　　(　　)

Unit 12 Scotland

(   )   (   )   (   )

(   )   (   )

(Haggis, Kilts, Nessie, Bagpipe, Tartan, Thistle, Caber-tossing, Scotch Whisky)

2. Scotland can be divided into three regions; they are _____, _____, and _____.
3. _____ is the capital of Scotland and _____ is the largest city.
4. **Group Work**: Form groups of three or four students. Try to find, on the Internet or in the library, more information about Scotland, for example, its landscape, its specialty, its legend, which interests you most. Get ready for a 5-minute presentation in class.

Start to Read

Text A   View of Scotland

Location

Scotland is a very small country. It is 274 miles (441 kilometers) long. The coastline is so **jagged** that it **adds up** to 2000 miles (3218 kilometers). At its widest point, it is 154 miles (248 kilometers). At its narrowest it is only 25 miles (40 kilometers). Because of Scotland's narrowness and its deep inlets, it is never possible to get far away from the sea.

Scotland occupies the northern third of the islands of Great Britain. The river Tweed and the Cheviot Hills form Scotland's southern border with England. The North Channel separates southwestern Scotland from Northern Ireland. The northwest coast faces the Atlantic Ocean. The east coast faces the North Sea, which separates Scotland from the mainland of Europe.

Composition

Scotland has three main land regions. They are, from north to south, the Highlands, the Central Lowlands, and the Southern Uplands.

1. The Highlands

The Highlands is a rugged, barren region that covers the northern two thirds of Scotland. There are two major mountain ranges; the North West Highlands and the Grampian Mountains rise in this region. The ranges have parallel ridges that run through the Highlands from northeast to southwest. A deep valley called Glen Mor or the Great Glen separates the two mountain ranges. The highest peak in the British Isle, Ben Nevis, which rises south of Glen Mor, is 4406 feet (1343 meters). The Highlands have two kinds of valleys: steep, narrow glens and broad, rolling straths. Much of the land in the Highlands is a treeless area called a moor or a heath. The most rugged land lies along the west coast. Most Highlanders live on the narrow coastal plains. And here you can visit the Cairngorms National Park.

2. The Central Lowlands

Loch Lomond and the Trossachs National Park is crossed by the Highland Boundary Fault, a break in the earth's crust which **occurred** millions of years ago. This line **defines** the border between the Lowlands and Highlands of Scotland, creating the diversity of landscape within the Park. The valleys of the Rivers Clyde, Forth, and Tay cross the Central Lowlands. This region has Scotland's best farmland. Wide, fertile fields and low hills with patches of trees cover the entire region. About three-fourths of Scottish people live in the lowlands.

3. The Southern Uplands

The Southern Uplands consist of rolling moors broken in places by rocky cliffs. The top of the hills are largely barren, but rich pasture land covers most of the lower slopes. Many sheep and cattle are raised in the southern uplands. In the south, the uplands rise to the Cheviot Hills.

Rivers and Lakes

The river Clyde is Scotland's most important river. Ships from the Atlantic Ocean can **sail up** the Clyde to Glasgow. The Clyde was narrow and shallow until the 1700's when engineers **widened** and **deepened** the river to make it navigable. Scotland's longest rivers flow eastward into the North Sea. The Tay, 120 miles (193 kilometers) long, is the largest river in Scotland. It carries more water than any other river in the United Kingdom. Many of Scotland's rivers flow into wide bays called Firths. The Firths of Forth, Tay, and Moray are on the east coast. The Firths of Clyde and Lorn lie on the west side. All ships **bound for** Glasgow must pass through the Firth of Clyde. A **suspension** bridge, one of the longest in the world, **spans** the Firth of Forth at Queens Ferry. It is 8244 feet (2313 meters) long.

Most of Scotland's lakes (which are called lochs) lie in deep Highland valleys. Loch Lomond is Scotland's largest lake. It is 23 miles (37 kilometers) long and 5 miles (8 kilometers) at its widest point. A series of lakes extend through Glen Mor. These lakes are connected by canals and form the

Caledonian Canal, which cuts across Scotland from Moray Firth to the Firth of Lorn. One of the lakes is famous for its "monster". (What's the name of this lake?) Some people claim to have seen a creature 30 feet (9 meters) long in the lake. Along the west coast of Scotland, the Atlantic Ocean extends inland in many narrow bays called sea lochs.

Islands

Scotland has hundreds of islands. A large group of islands called the Hebrides lie off the west coast of Scotland's mainland. The Orkney and Shetland groups lie north of the mainland and form the boundary between the North Sea and the Atlantic Ocean.

Cities

The major cities of Scotland, in order of size, are Glasgow, Edinburgh, Aberdeen and Dundee.

1. Edinburgh

Edinburgh is the capital of Scotland, its second largest city after Glasgow which is situated 45 miles (72 km) to the west, one of Scotland's 32 local government council areas and the seventh largest city in the United Kingdom.

Located in the southeast of Scotland, Edinburgh lies on the east coast of Scotland's Central Belt, along the Firth of Forth, near the North Sea. **Owing to** its rugged setting and vast collection of Medieval and Georgian architecture, including numerous stone tenements, it is often considered one of the most picturesque cities in Europe.

Edinburgh forms the City of Edinburgh council area; the city council area includes urban Edinburgh and a 30-square-mile (78 km) rural area. It has been the capital of Scotland since 1437 and is the seat of the Scottish Parliament. The city was one of the major centres of the **Enlightenment**, led by the University of Edinburgh, earning it the nickname "Athens of the North". The Old Town and New Town districts of Edinburgh were listed as a UNESCO World Heritage Site in 1995. There are over 4,500 listed buildings within the city. In the census of 2001, Edinburgh had a total resident population of 448,625.

Edinburgh is well-known for the annual Edinburgh Festival, a collection of official and independent festivals held annually over about four weeks from early August. The number of visitors attracted to Edinburgh for the Festival is roughly equal to the settled population of the city. The most famous of these events are the Edinburgh Fringe (the largest performing arts festival in the world), the Edinburgh International Festival, the Edinburgh Military Tattoo, the Edinburgh International Film Festival, and the Edinburgh International Book Festival.

The city is one of Europe's major tourist destinations, attracting around 13 million visitors a year, and is the second most visited tourist destination in the United Kingdom, after London.

2. Glasgow

Glasgow is the largest city in Scotland and third most **populous** in the United Kingdom. Fully named as the City of Glasgow, it is the most populous of Scotland's 32 unitary authority areas. The city is situated on the River Clyde in the country's west central lowlands. A person from Glasgow is known as a Glaswegian, which is also the name of the local dialect.

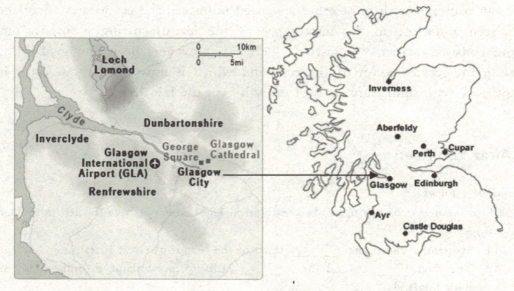

Glasgow grew from the medieval Bishopric of Glasgow and the later establishment of the University of Glasgow, which **contributed to** the Scottish Enlightenment. From the 18th century the city became one of Europe's main hubs of transatlantic trade with the Americas. With the Industrial Revolution, the city and surrounding region grew to become one of the world's pre-eminent centres of engineering and shipbuilding, constructing many revolutionary and famous vessels. Glasgow was known as the "Second City of the British Empire" in the Victorian era. Today it is one of Europe's top sixteen financial centres and is home to many of Scotland's leading businesses.

In the late 19th and early 20th centuries Glasgow grew to a population of over one million, and was the fourth-largest city in Europe, after London, Paris and Berlin. In the 1960s large-scale **relocation** to new towns and **peripheral** suburbs, followed by **successive** boundary changes, have reduced the current population of the City of Glasgow unitary authority area to 580,690.

Industry

Scotland was one of the industrial powerhouses of Europe from the time of the Industrial Revolution onwards, being a world leader in manufacturing and shipbuilding related industries, at the time, which today has left a **legacy** in the diversity of goods and services. The Scottish economy produces from textiles, whisky and shortbread to aeroengines, buses, computer software, ships, avionics and microprocessors to banking, insurance, fund management and other related financial services.

In common with most other advanced industrialized economies, Scotland has seen a decline in the importance of the manufacturing industries and primary-based **extractive** industries. This has, however, been **combined with** a rise in the service sector of the economy which is now the largest sector in Scotland, with significant rates of growth over the last decade.

After You Read

Knowledge Focus
1. **Fill in the blanks according to the geographical knowledge you have learned in the text above.**
    (1) Scotland occupies the _____ third of the islands of Great Britain.
    (2) The river _____ and the _____ Hills form Scotland's southern border with England.
    (3) The _____ separates southwestern Scotland from Northern Ireland.
    (4) The northwest coast faces _____. The east coast faces the North Sea, which separates Scotland from the mainland of _____.
    (5) Scotland has three main land regions. They are _____, the Central Lowlands, and _____.
    (6) The Highlands is a rugged, barren region that covers the _____ two thirds of Scotland. There are two major mountain ranges; the North West Highlands and _____ rise in this region.
    (7) The highest peak in the British Isle is _____.

(8) The river _____ is Scotland's most important river. _____ is the largest river in Scotland.
(9) _____ is Scotland's largest lake. _____ is famous for its monster.
(10) A large group of islands called the Hebrides lie off the _____ coast of Scotland's mainland. The Orkney and Shetland groups lie _____ of the mainland and form the boundary between the North Sea and the Atlantic Ocean.
(11) _____ is the largest city in Scotland, and _____ is the second largest and the capital.

2. **Write T in the brackets if the statement is true and write F if it is false.**
   (1) Located in the south-east of Scotland, Edinburgh lies on the west coast of Scotland's Central Belt, along the Firth of Forth, near the North Sea. ( )
   (2) Edinburgh is well-known for the annual Edinburgh Festival, a collection of official and independent festivals held annually over about four weeks from early August. ( )
   (3) Glasgow is the largest city in Scotland and second most populous in the United Kingdom. ( )
   (4) Glasgow was known as the "Second City of the British Empire" in the Elizabethan era. ( )
   (5) Scotland was one of the industrial powerhouses of Europe from the time of the Industrial Revolution onwards. ( )

Language Focus
1. **Fill in the blanks with the proper form of the phrases below.**

flow into	in order of	separate...from
add up to	be situated to	owing to
be equal to	grow from	

   (1) The coastline is so jagged that it _____ 2000 miles (3218 kilometers).
   (2) Edinburgh is the capital of Scotland and the second largest city after Glasgow which _____ 45 miles _____ the west.
   (3) _____ its rugged setting and vast collection of Medieval and Georgian architecture, including numerous stone tenements, it is often considered one of the most picturesque cities in Europe.
   (4) Many of Scotland's rivers _____ wide bays called Firths.
   (5) The North West Channel _____ southwestern Scotland _____ Northern Ireland.
   (6) The number of visitors attracted to Edinburgh for the Festival _____ the settled population of the city.
   (7) Glasgow _____ the medieval Bishopric of Glasgow and the later establishment of the University of Glasgow contributed to the Scottish Enlightenment.
   (8) The major cities of Scotland, _____ size, are Glasgow, Edinburgh, Aberdeen and Dundee.

2. **Fill in the blanks with the appropriate form of the words in the brackets.**
    (1) Because of Scotland's _____ (narrow) and its deep inlets, it is never possible to get far away from the sea.
    (2) The Highlands is a rugged, _____ (barrenness) region that covers the northern two thirds of Scotland.
    (3) Much of the land in the Highlands is a _____ (tree) area called a moor or a heath.
    (4) The Clyde was narrow and shallow until the 1700's when engineers widened and _____ (deep) the river to make it _____ (navigate).
    (5) A _____ (suspend) bridge, one of the longest in the world, spans the Firth of Forth at Queens Ferry.
    (6) Fully named as the City of Glasgow, it is the most _____ (populate) of Scotland's 32 unitary authority areas.
    (7) The later _____ (establish) of the University of Glasgow contributed to the Scottish _____ (enlight).
    (8) It is one of Europe's top sixteen _____ (finance) centres and is home to many of Scotland's _____ (lead) businesses.
    (9) In the 1960s large-scale _____ (relocate) to new towns and peripheral suburbs, followed by _____ (succeed) boundary changes, have reduced the current population of the City of Glasgow unitary authority area to 580,690.
    (10) Edinburgh is often considered one of the most _____ (picture) cities in Europe.
    (11) Edinburgh is well-known for the annual Edinburgh Festival, a collection of _____ (office) and _____ (independence) festivals held _____ (annual) over about four weeks from early August.

3. **Fill in the blanks with the proper prepositions and adverbs that collocate with the neighboring words.**
    (1) _____ its widest point, it is 154 miles (248 kilometers).
    (2) The ranges have parallel ridges that run _____ the Highlands from northeast to southwest.
    (3) Many sheep and cattle are raised _____ the southern uplands. In the south, the uplands rise _____ the Cheviot Hills.
    (4) Ships from the Atlantic Ocean can sail _____ the Clyde to Glasgow.
    (5) All ships bound for Glasgow must pass _____ the Firth of Clyde. A suspension bridge, one of the longest in the world, spans the Firth of Forth _____ Queens Ferry.
    (6) These lakes are connected by canals and form the Caledonian Canal, which cuts _____ Scotland from Moray Firth to the Firth of Lorn.
    (7) Located in the south-east of Scotland, Edinburgh lies _____ the east coast of Scotland's Central Belt, _____ the Firth of Forth, near the North Sea.
    (8) The city is one of Europe's major tourist destinations, attracting _____ 13 million visitors a year, and is the second most visited tourist destination in the

United Kingdom, _____ London.

(9) _____ common with most other advanced industrialised economies, Scotland has seen a decline _____ the importance of the manufacturing industries and primary-based extractive industries.

4. **Translate the following phrases into English. Pay attention to the attributive nouns.**
   (1) 一座吊桥
   (2) 一只咖啡杯
   (3) 一家服装店
   (4) 一辆跑车
   (5) 两名男护士
   (6) 三位女教师
   (7) 眼药水
   (8) 恐怖影片

Comprehensive Work

1. **Pair Work:**
   (1) Locate the important rivers, lakes, cities, its surrounding oceans, groups of islands on the map.
   (2) Give a brief introduction to Scotland in turn.

2. **Group Work:** Work in groups of three or four students. Try to complete the graph below.

Items	England	Scotland
Location		
Size		
Mountains/Hills		
Rivers		
Lakes		
Islands		
National Parks		

3. **Solo Work:** Which city do you prefer to visit, Edinburgh or Glasgow? Why? Write a composition within 300 words.

Read More

Text B Loch Ness

Read the passage quickly and try to find the information to fill in the blanks below.

(1) Loch Ness is located in the _____.
(2) It is best known for the alleged sightings of the legendary Loch Ness Monster called _____.
(3) It is the _____ largest Scottish Loch by surface area, but due to its great depth, it is the _____ by volume.
(4) Loch Ness's water visibility is exceptionally _____ due to a high _____ content in the surrounding soil.
(5) Cherry Island is the only island on _____; it is a crannog, a form of _____.

Loch Ness is a large, deep, freshwater loch in the Scottish Highlands extending for approximately 37 km (23 miles) southwest of Inverness. Its surface is 15.8 meters (52 feet) above sea level. Loch Ness is best known for the **alleged** sightings of the legendary Loch Ness Monster, also known as "Nessie". For many years it has been supposed that there is a large dinosaur-like "monster" resident in Loch Ness. The evidence for its existence are a series of sightings of a plesiosaur-like dinosaur throughout the last 100 years. The case has occasionally been supported by indistinct photographic evidence.

However, several scientific studies have been **conducted**, including thorough sonar surveys of the loch, and these have not **revealed** any presence of such a "monster". Many people believe that the size (21 square miles) and great depth of the loch (almost 800 feet), together with **potential** underwater caves, gives the monster many places to hide.

Regardless of the truth, the suggestion of the Monster's existence makes Loch Ness one of Scotland's top tourist attractions.

Loch Morar, in the West of Scotland, is also said to support a monster, but the evidence for this is even more **tenuous**!

Loch Ness is the second largest Scottish loch by surface area at 56.4 km (21.8 sq mi) after Loch Lomond, but due to its great depth is the largest by volume. Its deepest point is 230 m (754 feet), deeper than the height of London's BT (British Telecome) Tower at 189 m (620 feet) and deeper than any other loch besides Loch Morar. It contains more fresh water than all lakes in England and Wales combined, and is the largest body of water on the Great Glen geologic fault, which runs from Inverness in the north to Fort William in the south. The Caledonian Canal, which links the sea at either end of the fault, uses Loch Ness for part of its route. It is one of a series of **interconnected**, **murky** bodies of water in Scotland; its water visibility is exceptionally low due to a high peat content in the surrounding soil.

Loch Ness acts as the lower **storage** reservoir for the Foyers pumped-storage hydroelectric scheme, which was the first of its kind in the United Kingdom. The turbines were originally used to provide power for a nearby aluminium smelting plant, but now electricity is **generated** and supplied to the National Grid.

The only island on Loch Ness is Cherry Island, visible at its southwestern end, near Fort Augustus. It is a crannog, which is a form of artificial island. Most crannogs were constructed during the Iron Age.

At Drumnadrochit is the Loch Ness Exhibition Centre which examines the **controversy** through the natural history of Loch Ness. Boat cruises operate from various locations on the loch shore, giving visitors the chance to look for the monster.

Text C   Thistle: Scotland's National Flower

Read the passage and finish the following multiple-choice questions.

(1) Hundreds of years ago, the Romans _____.
   A. came from the north through England to make war on Scotland
   B. came to the north Scotland from England to make war on Scotland
   C. came from the north of England to fight the Scots
   D. came to the north from the south of Britain to fight the Scots

(2) At the shout of a Roman soldier, all the Scots who were asleep at the hill _____.
   A. began to fight the Romans hard
   B. stood up without putting on their shoes and began to fight
   C. woke and rose immediately, ready to fight
   D. put their feet into their shoes at once and were ready to fight

(3) The result of the war is that _____.
   A. the Romans killed all the Scots
   B. the Scots were defeated
   C. the Scots were driven out of Scotland
   D. the Scots defeated the Romans
(4) The Scots made thistle their national flower because thistle _____.
   A. is lovely, though not beautiful
   B. gave them happiness
   C. is a kind of useful plant
   D. helped the Scots in wiping out the Romans

Hundreds of years ago, a Roman army came north from England to make war on Scotland. The Scots, a brave people, love their country. They fought hard to drive the enemy out of Scotland. But there were too many of the Romans. It looked as if the Romans would win.

One night, the leader of the Scots marched his soldiers to the top of a hill. "We will rest here tonight, my men," he said, "Tomorrow we will fight one more battle. We must win, or we will die."

They were all very tired. So they ate their supper quickly and fell asleep. There were four guards on duty, but they were very tired, too, and one by one, they fell asleep.

The Romans were not asleep. Quickly they gathered at the foot of the hill. Slowly they went up the hill. Closer they came to the sleeping Scots. They were almost at the top. A few minutes more the war would be over. Suddenly, one of them put his foot on a thistle. He cried out and his sudden cry woke the Scots. In a minute they were on their feet and ready for a battle. The fighting was hard, but it did not last long. The Scots wiped out the Romans and saved Scotland.

The thistle is not a beautiful plant. It has sharp needles all over it. Few people liked it. But the people of Scotland liked it so much that they made it their national flower.

Unit 12 Scotland

Proper Nouns

Aberdeen 阿伯丁
Athens of the North 北部雅典（爱丁堡的别称）
Ben Nevis 本内维斯山
BT (British Telecome) Tower 伦敦电讯大楼
Drumnadrochit 庄娜村
Dundee 敦提
Edinburgh 爱丁堡
Edinburgh Castle 爱丁堡城堡
Fort Augustus 奥古斯都堡
Fort William 威廉堡市
Glasgow 格拉斯哥
Glaswegian 格拉斯哥人
Glen Mor or the Great Glen 莫尔峡谷
Georgian architecture 佐治亚时代建筑
Inverness 印威内斯市
Loch Lomond 罗蒙湖
Loch Lomond and the Trossachs National Park 罗蒙湖和特罗萨克斯国家公园
Loch Morar 摩拉湖
Loch Ness Monster (Nessie) 尼斯湖水怪
Moray (Firth) 摩里湾
Orkney 奥克尼郡
Queens Ferry 皇后码头
Scotland's Central Belt 苏格兰中部地带
Second City of the British Empire 大英帝国第二大城市（旧时格拉斯哥的别称）
Shetland 设得兰岛
the Caledonian Canal 喀里多尼亚运河
the Cairngorms National Park 凯恩戈姆国家公园
the Central Lowlands 苏格兰东南部低地
the Cheviot Hills 切维厄特丘陵
the City of Edinburgh 爱丁堡城
the City of Glasgow 格拉斯哥城
the Edinburgh Festival 爱丁堡艺术节
the Edinburgh Fringe 爱丁堡边缘艺术节
the Edinburgh International Book Festival 爱丁堡国际图书节
the Edinburgh International Festival 爱丁堡国际艺术节
the Edinburgh International Film Festival 爱丁堡国际电影节
the Edinburgh Military Tattoo 爱丁堡军乐节
the Enlightenment 启蒙运动
the Firth of Forth 福斯河口
the Firth of Lorn 罗恩湾
the Foyers 福耶斯电站
the Great Glen geologic fault 大峡谷断层/大格兰断层
the Hebrides 赫布里底群岛
the Highland Boundary Fault 高地边界断层
the Highlands 高地
the Jazz and Blues Festival 爵士乐蓝调节
the Loch Ness Exhibition Centre 尼斯湖展览中心
the medieval Bishopric 主教辖区
the National Grid 英国国家电网/英国国家电力供应公司
the North Channel 北海峡
the North Sea 北海
the North West Highlands 西北高地
the Rivers Clyde 克莱德河
the River Tay 泰河
the Scottish Parliament 苏格兰国会
the Southern Uplands 南部高地
the University of Edinburgh 爱丁堡大学
the Victorian era 维多利亚女王时代
UNESCO World Heritage Site 联合国教科文组织世界遗产遗址

For Fun

Books to read

Scottish Fairy Tales by Donald A. Mackenzie

   The eight Scottish fairy tales contained in this paperback are delightful adventures.

Virtues such as loyalty, honesty, and wisdom are the characteristics of even the least of heroes. This Dover edition, first published in 1997, is a new selection of fairy tales from "Wonder Tales from Scottish Myth and Legend", originally published by Frederick A. Stokes Co., New York, in 1917. John Green provides illustrations specifically for this edition. The tales are: "Battle of the Fairy Kings", "The Princess of Land-under-Waves", "Conall and the Thunder Hag", "The Story of Finlay and the Giants", "The Story of Michael Scott", "In the Kingdom of Seals", "The Maid-of-the-Wave", and "The Land of Green Mountains". This is indeed an excellent read.

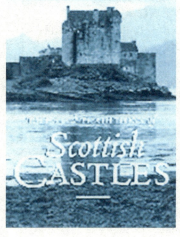

Tales and Traditions of Scottish Castles by Nigel G. Tranter

Nigel Tranter's gift for bringing Scottish history to life is demonstrated in this lively book, which details 45 of the nation's castles with their associated tales and traditions. With a broad geographical spread, Tranter breathes life into many of Scotland's gaunt and shadowy ruins with a lively mix of anecdote, fact, myth, and legend. It is an essential holiday companion when visiting Scotland.

Movies to see

Braveheart (1995)

In 14th Century Scotland, William Wallace leads his people in a rebellion against the tyranny of the English King, who has given English nobility the "Prima Nocta", a right to take all new brides for the first night. The Scots are none too pleased with the brutal English invaders, but they lack leadership to fight back. Wallace creates a legend of himself, with his courageous defence of his people and attacks on the English.

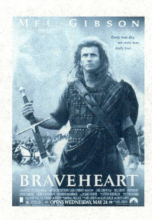

Sweet Sixteen (2002)

It is a 2002 film by director Ken Loach. The film tells the story of a working class

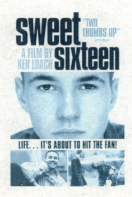

Scottish teenage boy, Liam (played by Martin Compston), a typical "ned", who dreams of starting afresh with his mother who is completing a prison term. Liam's attempts to raise money for the two of them are set against the backdrop of Greenock and Port Glasgow.

Mary, Queen of Scots (1971)

Mary Stuart, who was named Queen of Scotland when she was only six days old, is the last Roman Catholic ruler of Scotland. She is imprisoned at he age of 23 by her cousin Elizabeth Tudor, the English Queen and her arch adversary. Nineteen years later the life of Mary is to be ended on the scaffold and with her execution the last threat to Elizabeth's throne has been removed. The two Queens with their contrasting personalities make a dramatic counterpoint to history.

Songs to enjoy

Flower of Scotland

By Roy Williamson et al.

It is a popular Scottish song, used frequently at special occasions and sporting events. Although Scotland has no official national anthem, *Flower of Scotland* is one of a number of songs which unofficially fulfill this role, along with *Highland Cathedral* and the older *Scotland the Brave*.

O Flower of Scotland,
When will we see
Your like again,
That fought and died for,
Your wee bit Hill and Glen,
And stood against him,
Proud Edward's army,
And sent him homeward,
Tae think again.

The hills are bare now,
And autumn leaves
lie thick and still,
O'er land that is lost now,
Which those so dearly held,
That stood against him,
Proud Edward's Army,
And sent him homeward,

Tae think again.

Those days are past now,
And in the past
they must remain,
But we can still rise now,
And be the nation again,
That stood against him,
Proud Edward's Army,
And sent him homeward,
Tae think again.

O Flower of Scotland,
When will we see
your like again,
That fought and died for,
Your wee bit Hill and Glen,
And stood against him,
Proud Edward's Army,
And sent him homeward,
Tae think again.

(*Flower of Scotland* is played at rugby and football games. However, athletes celebrate medals with *Scotland the Brave*.)

Scotland the Brave
Composed by Cliff Hanley

Hark when the night is falling,
Hear! Hear the pipes are calling,
Loudly and proudly calling down through the glen.
There where the hills are sleeping,
now feel the blood a leaping,
High as the spirits of the old highland men.
Towering in gallant frame,
Scotland my mountain hame
High may your proud standards gloriously wave.
Land of my high endeavour,
land of the shining river,
Land of my heart forever,
Scotland the Brave.

High in the misty highlands,
out by the purple islands,
Brave are the hearts that beat beneath Scottish skies.
Wild are the winds to meet you,
staunch are the friends that greet you,
Kind as the love that shines from fair maiden's eyes.

Towering in gallant frame,
Scotland my mountain hame
High may your proud standards gloriously wave.
Land of my high endeavour,
land of the shining river,
Land of my heart forever,
Scotland the Brave.

Far off in sunlit places,
sad are the Scottish faces,
Yearning to feel the kiss of sweet Scottish rain.
Where tropics skies are beaming,
love sets the heart a dreaming,
Longing and dreaming of the homeland again.
Towering in gallant frame,
Scotland my mountain hame
High may your proud standards gloriously wave.
Land of my high endeavour,
land of the shining river,
Land of my heart forever,
Scotland the Brave.

Unit 13
Wales

> Each section of the British Isles has its own way of laughing, except Wales, which doesn't.
> —Stephen Leacock

Unit Goals

- To have a general idea of the geography of Wales
- To be familiar with the geographical terms about Wales
- To be able to introduce Wales
- To be able to describe the Seven Wonders, Cardiff and Et David's Day
- To be able to compare and contrast Scotland and Wales
- To be able to use "use" properly

Before You Read

1. Which of the following is the flag of Wales? How about the other one?

2. The _____ is one of the national emblems of _____, whose citizens wear it—or the daffodil—on St. David's Day.

151

3. _____ is the capital and largest city in Wales and the tenth largest city in the United kingdom.

4. **Group Work**: Form groups of three or four students. Try to find, on the Internet or in the library, more information about Wales, for example, its landscape, its specialty, its legend, which interests you most. Get ready for a 5-minute presentation in class.

Start to Read

Text A   View of Wales

Physical Characteristics

Wales is a **constituent** country of the United Kingdom of Great Britain and Northern Ireland. It is located on a peninsula in central-west Great Britain. Its area, the size of Wales, is about 20,779 km² (about a quarter of the size of Scotland). Wales is bordered by England to the east and by sea in the other three directions: Bristol Channel to the south, St. George's Channel to the west, and the Irish Sea to the north. Altogether, Wales has over 1,200 km of coastline. There are several islands off the Welsh mainland, the largest being Anglesey in the northwest. Wales has a population estimated at three million and is a **bilingual** country, with English the language spoken by the majority, and Welsh the native tongue.

Landscape

Much of Wales' diverse landscape is mountainous, particularly in the north and central regions. The mountains were shaped during the last ice age. The highest mountains in Wales are in Snowdonia, and include Snowdon, which, at 1085 m (3,560 ft) is the highest peak in Wales. The 14 (or possibly 15) Welsh mountains over 3,000 feet high are known **collectively** as the Welsh 3000s. The Brecon Beacons are in the south, and are joined by the Cambrian Mountains in Mid Wales.

Wales has three National Parks: Snowdonia, Brecon Beacons and Pembrokeshire Coast. It also has five Areas of Outstanding Natural Beauty. These areas include Anglesey, the Clwydian Range, the Gower peninsula, the Llyn peninsula and the Wye Valley. The Gower peninsula was the first area in the whole of the United Kingdom to be designated as an Area of Outstanding Natural Beauty, in 1956.

The Seven Wonders of Wales is a list in doggerel verse of seven geographic and cultural landmarks in Wales probably **composed** in the late 18th century under the influence of tourism from England. All the "wonders" are in north Wales: Snowdon (the highest mountain), the Gresford bells (the peal of bells in the medieval church of All Saints at Gresford), the Llangollen Bridge (built in 1347 over the River Dee, Afon Dyfrdwy), St Winefride's Well (a pilgrimage site at Holywell, Treffynnon in Flintshire), the Wrexham (Wrecsam) steeple (16th century tower of St. Giles Church in Wrexham), the Overton yew trees (ancient yew trees in the churchyard of St. Mary's at Overton-on-Dee) and Pistyll Rhaeadr (Wales' tallest waterfall, at 240 ft). The wonders are part of the rhyme:

> Pistyll Rhaeadr and Wrexham steeple,
> Snowdon's mountain without its people,
> Overton yew trees, St Winefride's Wells,
> Llangollen Bridge and Gresford bells.

Capital

Official capital of Wales since only 1955, the **buoyant** city of Cardiff has **swiftly** grown into its new status. A number of **progressive** developments, not least the new, sixty-member Welsh National Assembly, are giving the city the feel of an international capital, if not always a very Welsh one: compared with Swansea, Cardiff is very **anglicized**—you'll rarely hear Welsh on the city's streets.

The second Marquis of Bute built Cardiff's first dock in 1839, opening others in swift **succession**. The Butes, who owned **massive** swathes of the rapidly industrializing South Wales valleys, **insisted** that all coal and iron exports use the family docks in Cardiff, and it became one of the busiest ports in the world. In the hundred years up to the turn of the twentieth century, Cardiff's population had **soared** from almost nothing to 170,000, and the **spacious** and **ambitious** new civic centre in Cathays Park was well under way. The twentieth century **saw** varying **fortunes**: the dock trade **slumped** in the 1930s and the city suffered heavy bombing in World War II, but with the creation of Cardiff as capital in 1955, **optimism** and confidence in the city have **blossomed**. Many large governmental and media institutions have moved here from London, and the development of the dock areas around the new Assembly building to be built in Cardiff Bay has given a largely positive **boost** to the cityscape.

Agriculture and Industry

Wales is a land of small farms. Sheep farming is predominant in the mountains and moorlands, dairy and mixed farming around the coast. Wales' industry has changed **drastically** over the last hundred years. At the turn of the 20th century, the emphasis was on coal and steel in the south and slate in the north. The transport of these items **gave rise to** a strong maritime industry too.

Coal exports, manufacturing and heavy industry have declined nowadays and have been replaced by new industries. Tourism and public services have **taken over** as the main employers within Wales.

The shape of manufacturing has also changed. The traditional heavy industries have **given way to** lighter manufacturing such as electronics, parts and technology. Unemployment in Wales is higher than in both Scotland and England and wages are on average lower.

British governments have attracted English and multi-national companies to Wales with **generous incentives**. However, recent years have seen a strong growth in the science and technology sectors. So this may change.

After You Read

Knowledge Focus

1. **Fill in the blanks according to the geographical knowledge you have learned in the text above.**

    (1) Wales is a constituent country of _____. It is located on a peninsula in central-_____ Great Britain.

    (2) Wales is bordered by _____ to the east and by sea in the other three directions:

_____ to the south, St. George's Channel to the west, and _____ to the north.

(3) There are several islands off the Welsh mainland, the largest being _____ in the northwest.

(4) Much of Wales' diverse landscape is _____, particularly in the north and central regions.

(5) _____, at 1085 m (3,560 ft), is the highest peak in Wales.

(6) Wales has three National Parks: _____, _____ and Pembrokeshire Coast.

(7) Wales has five _____. _____ was the first area in the whole of the United Kingdom to be designated as an Area of Outstanding Natural Beauty, in 1956.

(8) _____ of Wales is a list in doggerel verse of seven geographic and cultural landmarks in Wales.

(9) The capital of Wales is the city of _____.

2. **Write T in the brackets if the statement is true and write F if it is false.**

(1) Wales is located on a peninsula in central-east Great Britain. ( )

(2) Wales is bordered by England to the east and by sea in the other three directions: Bristol Channel to the north, St. George's Channel to the west, and the Irish Sea to the south. ( )

(3) The Gower peninsula was the first area in the whole of the United Kingdom to be designated as an Area of Outstanding Natural Beauty, in 1956. ( )

(4) The Seven Wonders of Wales is a list in doggerel verse of seven geographic and cultural landmarks in Wales probably composed in the late 18th century under the influence of tourism from England. ( )

(5) All the "wonders" are in south Wales: Snowdon, the Gresford bells, the Llangollen bridge, St Winefride's Well, the Wrexham steeple, the Overton Yew trees, and Pistyll Rhaeadr. ( )

(6) Cardiff is a very anglicized city, you'll rarely hear Welsh on the city's streets. ( )

(7) After the creation of Cardiff as capital in 1955, many large governmental and media institutions have moved here from London. ( )

Language Focus

1. **Fill in the blanks with the proper form of the phrases below.**

| on average | under way | native tongue | under the influence of |
| in succession | be known as | compare with | be predominant in |

(1) Wales is a bilingual country, with English the language spoken by the majority, and Welsh the _____.

(2) This poem was probably composed in the late 18th century _____ tourism from England.

(3) Unemployment in Wales is higher than in both Scotland and England and wages are _____ lower.

(4) _____ Swansea, Cardiff is very anglicized—you'll rarely hear Welsh on the city's streets.
(5) Sheep farming _____ the mountains and moorlands, dairy and mixed farming around the coast.
(6) In the hundred years up to the turn of the twentieth century, and the spacious and ambitious new civic centre in Cathays Park was well _____.
(7) The 14 Welsh mountains over 3,000 feet high _____ the Welsh 3000s.
(8) The second Marquis of Bute built Cardiff's first dock in 1839, opening others _____.

2. **Fill in the blanks with the appropriate form of the words in the brackets.**
   (1) Wales is a _____ (constitute) country of the United Kingdom of Great Britain and Northern Ireland.
   (2) Wales has a population estimated at three million and is a bilingual country, with English the language spoken by the _____ (major), and Welsh the native tongue.
   (3) The doggerel verse was probably _____ (composition) in the late 18th century under the influence of _____ (tourist) from England.
   (4) Official capital of Wales since only 1955, the _____ (buoyancy) city of Cardiff has _____ (swift) grown into its new status.
   (5) A number of _____ (progress) developments are giving the city the feel of an international capital, if not always a very _____ (Wales) one.
   (6) The second Marquis of Bute built Cardiff's first dock in 1839, opening others in swift _____ (succeed).
   (7) The Butes, who owned _____ (mass) swathes of the rapidly industrializing South Wales valleys, _____ (insistence) that all coal and iron exports use the family docks in Cardiff.
   (8) The _____ (space) and _____ (ambition) new civic centre in Cathays Park was well under way.
   (9) With the _____ (create) of Cardiff as capital in 1955, _____ (optimist) and _____ (confident) in the city have blossomed.

3. **Fill in the blanks with the proper prepositions and adverbs that collocate with the neighboring words.**
   (1) Wales is bordered _____ England to the east and by sea in the other three directions.
   (2) Altogether, Wales has _____ 1,200 km of coastline.
   (3) Wales has a population estimated _____ three million.
   (4) Wales is located _____ a peninsula in central-west Great Britain.
   (5) The Brecon Beacons are in the south, and are joined _____ the Cambrian Mountains in Mid Wales.
   (6) The mountains were shaped _____ the last ice age.
   (7) Cardiff's population had soared _____ almost nothing _____ 170,000.

(8) British governments have attracted English and multi-national companies _____ Wales with generous incentives.

4. **Fill in the blanks with the proper forms of "use".**
    (1) The Butes insisted that all coal and iron exports _____ the family docks in Cardiff.
    (2) The Tower Bridge _____ be raised about 50 times a day, but nowadays it is only raised 4 to 5 times a week.
    (3) Sometimes England _____ wrongly in reference to the whole UK.
    (4) Cornwall _____ be famous for its tin mines, which operated from Roman times until the last mine closed in 1998.
    (5) In the past, the ford _____ by cattle farmers to drive their oxen to market.
    (6) They _____ go camping every summer when they were students, _____ they?
    (7) After three weeks he had got _____ the extreme heat there.
    (8) He _____ glancing over newspapers after supper.

Comprehensive Work

1. **Pair Work:** What does the following map of Wales show? Do you know their names?

2. **Pair Work:** Discuss the following questions about the cartoon with your partner.
    (1) Where is it?
    (2) Who is the man?
    (3) What is he going to do?
    (4) What does the sentence "This is the only way I'll get a crown." mean?

This is the only way I'll get a crown

3. **Solo Work:** Write an essay or a poem illustrating the differences between Wales and Scotland.

Read More

Text B Legends of Wales

Read the passage quickly and fill in the blanks below.

(1) The red dragon is a symbol of _____ and _____ for the _____ people since the _____.

(2) _____ is the Patron saint of _____ and her people. On _____, _____ Day is celebrated as the national day of thanksgiving, women wearing a _____ and the men wearing a _____.

The legends and myths of Wales are so numerous that it would take years to tell all the stories. All the legends and myths have been told through the centuries by one generation to the next, and with question bits have been added to the stories, and some bits taken away. But what remains consistent is all the legends and myths have their base in history and fact. It is this history and fact that makes the stories so much a part of the Welsh culture, and gives it a proud and unique heritage to stand upon.

The Red Dragon

The red dragon has long been an emblem associated with the country of Wales. It is the mark of bravery and victory, and has been a symbol for the Welsh people since the Middle Ages. The dragon graces shields and standards and is part of many families crest or coat of arms.

When King Henry VII was crowned as the King of England in 1485, it is said that he ordered the Red Dragon become part of the official flag of the principality of Wales. And the Welsh are fiercely proud of their Dragon. "Y Ddraig Goch a ddyry Gychwyn"—the Red Dragon will show the way. And he most certainly has!

The Legend of St. David

St. David grew up in Ceredigion and kept company with monk, learning their ways and the Bible. David learned at the hand of a blind teacher named Paulinus, and it was due to this teacher that David discovered his gift for helping people. He laid his hands over the eyes of the teacher and restored his sight. David then began to travel throughout Wales, sharing his gift. It is said that while David was speaking to a flock of the faithful, he was not able to be heard or seen by all who had come to listen. And because of this problem the ground rose up and lifted him to heights where he could be seen and heard by all.

God came to David and told him to build a monastery in the Glyn Rhoysn valley. This is where St. David's Cathedral is located, on the grounds of the old monastery. St. David is the Patron saint of Wales and her people and he died on March 1. This is St. David's Day in Wales and is celebrated every year. This is celebrated every year as the national day of thanksgiving, and is traditionally signified by women wearing a daffodil and the men wearing a leek, both of which are Welsh National symbols.

Proper Nouns

Afon Dyfrdwy 迪河(威尔士语)
Anglesey 安格尔西岛
Cardiff 卡迪夫
Cardiff Bay 卡迪夫海湾
Cathays Park 凯西公园
Ceredigion 锡尔迪金郡
Flintshire 弗林特郡
Holywell 霍利威尔
Marquis of Bute 布特侯爵
Pembrokeshire Coast 彭布鲁克海岸国家公园
Snowdon 斯诺顿/雪顿峰
Snowdonia 斯诺多尼亚/雪顿国家公园
St. George's Channel 圣乔治海峡
St. Giles Church 圣吉尔斯教堂
St. Mary's 圣玛丽大教堂

St. Winefride's Well 圣温妮费德水井
Swansea 斯旺西
the Brecon Beacons 布雷肯-比肯山国家公园
the Clwydian Range 克卢迪安山脉
the Gower peninsula 高尔半岛
the Gresford bells 格雷斯福德钟声
the Llangollen Bridge 兰戈伦桥
the Overton yew trees 奥弗顿紫杉树
the Pistyll Rhaeadr 瀑布的春天
the River Dec 迪河
the Seven Wonders of Wales 威尔士七大奇观
the Wrexham (Wrecsam) steeple 雷瑟汉姆尖塔
Treffynnon 霍利威尔(威尔士语)
Welsh National Assembly 威尔士国民议会

For Fun

Websites to visit
http://en.wikipedia.org/wiki/Wales
　This is a webpage about Wales, on which you can find information on its history, governance, law, geography, economy, transport, culture, healthcare etc.
http://en.wikipedia.org/wiki/Cardiff
　This is a webpage about the Cardiff, on which you can find information on the history, governance, geography, demography, economy, culture, landmarks etc.

Book to read
Border Country by Raymond Williams

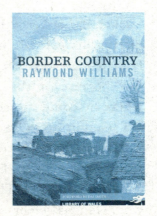

Matthew Price, a university lecturer in economic history, returns from London to visit his sick father in South Wales. The novel is set in the fictional village of Glynmawr in the Black Mountains, a rural area but closely connected to the nearby coal mining valleys of the South Wales coalfield. His father had been a railway signalman, and the story includes lengthy flashbacks to the 1920s and 1930s, including the General Strike and its impact on a small group of railway workers living in a community made up mostly of farmers. It also describes Matthew Price's decision to leave his own community, studying at Cambridge before becoming a lecturer in London.

Movie to see
The Englishman Who Went Up a Hill But Came Down a Mountain (1995)

Two English cartographers visit the small South Wales village of Ffynnon Garw, to measure what is claimed to be the "first mountain inside of Wales". It is 1917, and the war in Europe continues. The villagers are very proud of their "mountain", and are understandably disappointed and furious to find that it is in fact a "hill". Not to be outwitted by a rule (and the Englishmen who enforce it), the villagers set out to make their hill into a mountain, but to do so they must keep the English from leaving, before the job is done.

Song to enjoy
Land of My Fathers

"Hen Wlad Fy Nhadau" usually translated as "Land of My Fathers", is, by tradition, the national anthem of Wales. The words were written by Evan James and the tune composed by his son, James James.

Here is a translation from the Welsh.

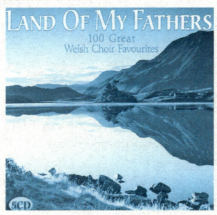

The old land of my fathers is dear to me,
Land of poets and singers, famous men of renown;
Her brave warriors, very splendid patriots,
For freedom shed their blood.

Nation [or country], Nation, I pledge to my Nation.
While the sea [is] a wall to the pure, most loved land,
O may the old language [sc. Cymraeg] endure.

Old mountainous Wales, paradise of the bard,
Every valley, every cliff, to me is beautiful.
Through patriotic feeling, so charming is the murmur
Of her brooks, rivers, to me.

If the enemy oppresses my land under his foot,
The old language of the Welsh is as alive as ever.
The muse is not hindered by the hideous hand of treason,
Nor [is] the melodious harp of my country.

Unit 14
Northern Ireland

> Anyone who isn't confused here doesn't really understand what is going on.
> —Belfast citizen quoted in the *Times*, April 1970

Unit Goals

- To have a general idea of the geography of Northern Ireland
- To be familiar with the geographical terms about Northern Ireland
- To be able to introduce Northern Ireland
- To be able to describe the Giant's Causeway, Belfast and St. Patrick's Day
- To be able to use "it" as a preparatory subject more skillfully

Before You Read

1. Northern Ireland is a country of _____. It is located on the Island of _____. It comprises about _____-sixth of the entire island.
2. _____, located in Northern Ireland, is the largest lake in British Isles.
3. Do you know what the photo on the right shows? It is one of the famous sights in _____. Have you ever heard any legends about it?
4. _____ is celebrated, for _____, one of the patron saints of Ireland, worldwide by those of Irish descent and increasingly by non-Irish people. The day is the national holiday of Ireland. It is a bank holiday in Northern Ireland and a public holiday in the Republic of Ireland.

5. **Group Work**: Form groups of three or four students. Try to find, on the Internet or in the library, more information about Northern Ireland, for example, its landscape, its specialty, its legend, which interests you most. Get ready for a 5-minute presentation in class.

Start to Read

Text A **View of Northern Ireland**

Location and Size

Northern Ireland is an integral part of the United Kingdom. It is situated in the northeastern portion of the island of Ireland. It is known as Ulster because it consists of six of the nine counties that were parts of the former province of Ulster. Belfast is the Capital City and the Seat of Government. It comprises about one-sixth of the entire island with 5,463 square miles (14,148 square kilometers), whereas the entire island consists of 32,595 square miles (84,431 square kilometers). The measurements of the island are 174 miles (280 kilometers) in width, and 302 miles (486 kilometers) in length. Northern Ireland measures about 85 miles (135 kilometers) north and south, and about 110 miles (175 kilometers) east and west. There is a spot in Northern Ireland that is only thirteen and one-half miles from

Scotland, although most sea crossings were fifty miles in the southern part of the island and 70 miles in the northern part.

Landscape

The shorelines of Northern Ireland (NI) are characterized by many **irregularities**. It consists of mountains surrounding Lough Neagh (about 150 square miles/390 square kilometers) on its northwest, northeast, and southeast. Lough Neagh is the largest lake in the British Isles. The highest point in the country is Slieve  Donard, a peak in the Mourne Mountains; it is 2796 feet/852 meters tall. For its small area, Northern Ireland has a great variety of scenic countryside although there are no National Parks. Large areas of landscape of distinctive character and special scenic value have been designated Areas of Outstanding Natural Beauty.

 The Giant's Causeway is an area of about 40,000 **interlocking** basalt columns, the result of an ancient **volcanic eruption**. It is located on the northeast coast of Ireland. It was declared a World Heritage Site by UNESCO in 1986. In a 2005 poll of *Radio Times* readers, the Giant's Causeway was named as the fourth greatest natural wonder in the United Kingdom. The tops of the columns form stepping stones that lead from the cliff foot and disappear under the sea. Most of the columns are hexagonal, although there are also some with four, five, seven and eight sides. The tallest are about 12 metres (36 ft) high, and the **solidified** lava in the cliffs is 28 metres thick in places. The Giant's Causeway is today owned and managed by the National Trust and it is the most popular tourist attraction in Northern Ireland.

Capital

For those who grew up in the 1970s and 1980s when Belfast was **plagued** by violence and political unrest, to think of it now **in terms of** tourism rather than terrorism requires some mental calisthenics. But try. Because this is an **extraordinary** time to visit this city, as it is still in the process of **picking** itself **up** and **dusting** itself **off** after years of strife. Nearly half a million people, a third of Northern Ireland's population, live in Belfast, most of them in neighborhoods **segregated** by religion. Yet, you really see little sign of any **residual** religious **tension** in the city center. In recent years, the center has been **polished up**, and it is a pleasure to wander its pedestrianized lanes, to shop in the **upscale** arcades **lined with** glittering jewelry stores and colorful boutiques, to **linger** in the historic pubs and to dine in the Michelin-starred restaurants.

The city is easily divided into **walkable** quarters: The City Center spreads out from around the impressive, domed City Hall building and bustling Donegall Square. This is the best place for shopping, particularly along Donegall Place, which extends north from the square, onto Royal Avenue. Bedford Street, which travels south from the Donegall Square, becomes Dublin Road, which, in turn, leads south to the University Quarter, the leafy area around Queen's University. This is where you'll find the Botanic Gardens, art galleries, and museums, as well as a **buzzing** nightlife scene. Heading north from Donegall Place, it is a short distance to the Cathedral Quarter, which surrounds Donegall Street, and holds, as the name **implies**, the city's most important cathedrals, as well as many vast Victorian warehouses. Finally there is the Golden Mile—the area around Great Victoria Street beyond Bradbury Place. It is considered the city's best address for restaurants and pubs, although it is a bit **hyperbolically** named. As one local said to me, "It's not a mile and it's not golden. But it's nice enough."

It is easiest to start in the center and then branch out from there. Perhaps tour the City Hall, then spend some time shopping for linen and china, then take a walk to the Cathedral Quarter to take in the architecture, and finally have dinner and drinks on the Golden Mile.

The **sectarian** areas, with the famous I.R.A. and Protestant murals, are just to the west of the city center. The most famous of these are on the Shankill and Falls roads. It is perfectly safe to drive the roads and take photos yourself (locals are quite proud of the murals), or you could take one of the Black Cab tours if you want a guide to explain what it all means.

Industry

NI's economy consists of the following: agriculture and forestry, fisheries, tourism, industry—linens, ropeworks, and clothing, mining and power, trade and finance, and transport and communications. Being the most industrialized part of the island, NI supports one-third of the island's total population. With 80% of the land still in farmland, NI is still the poorest part of the United Kingdom. In 1986, Northern Ireland had a high unemployment rate of around 21 percent.

Large shipyards are located in Belfast. In the earlier 1900s, NI was one of Britain's main shipping routes. Belfast constructed 600,000 tons of merchant shipping, one-tenth of the output of the whole United Kingdom. This includes the building of 6 aircraft carriers, 3 cruisers and several other large ships, making a total of 140 warships of all sizes and 123 merchant ships. Due to this, Belfast was the target of several destructive air raids during WWII. It was a landing place for United States forces. It has very valuable key agricultural and industrial resources of the province. This is why NI is of such strategic importance.

Most of the country's trade is with Great Britain, about 80% of it. The British pound is the legal tender. Exports consist of linen goods, textiles, clothing, machinery, and food—mainly meat, potatoes, and dairy products. Imports consist of petroleum, and other fuels, raw materials and metals, produce, and various manufactured goods.

Daily steamship and airline services connect NI with the rest of the world. Motorways and railways transport people and goods about the country. There are three newspapers in NI: *Belfast Telegraph*, *Irish News*, and *News Letter*. Combined circulation is about 272,000.

After You Read

Knowledge Focus

1. **Fill in the blanks according to the geographical knowledge you have learned in the text above.**

    (1) Northern Ireland is situated in the _____ portion of the island of Ireland. It is known as _____, because it consists of six of the nine counties that were parts

of the former province of Ulster.

(2) _____ is the Capital City and the Seat of Government.

(3) _____ is the largest lake in the British Isles. The highest point in the country is Slieve Donard, a peak in the _____.

(4) Large areas of landscape of distinctive character and special scenic value in Northern Ireland have been designated _____.

(5) With 80% of the land still in _____, NI is still the poorest part of the United Kingdom.

(6) Most of the country's trade is with _____, about 80% of it. The British _____ is the legal tender.

2. **Write T in the brackets if the statement is true and write F if it is false.**

(1) Northern Ireland is an integral part of the United Kingdom. It is situated in the northwestern portion of the island of Ireland. ( )

(2) Northern Ireland comprises about one-sixth of the entire island of Ireland. ( )

(3) In a 2005 poll of *Radio Times* readers, the Giant's Causeway was named as the greatest natural wonder in the United Kingdom. ( )

(4) Nearly half a million people, a third of Northern Ireland's population, live in Belfast, most of them in neighborhoods segregated by race. ( )

(5) NI's economy consists of the following: agriculture and forestry, fisheries, tourism, industry—linens, ropeworks, and clothing, mining and power, trade and finance, and transport and communications. ( )

(6) Most of Northern Ireland's trade is with Great Britain, about 80% of it. ( )

(7) There are three newspapers in NI: Belfast News, Irish News, and News Letter. Combined circulation is about 272,000. ( )

Language Focus

1. **Fill in the blanks with the proper form of the phrases below.**

| spread out | in terms of | consist of | as well as |
| due to | be named as | branch out | be situated in |

(1) In the earlier 1900s, NI was one of Britain's main shipping routes. _____ this, Belfast was the target of several destructive air raids during WWII.

(2) The City Center _____ from around the impressive, domed City Hall building and bustling Donegall Square.

(3) It is known as Ulster because it _____ six of the nine counties that were parts of the former province of Ulster.

(4) For those who grew up in the 1970s and 1980s when Belfast was plagued by violence and political unrest, to think of it now _____ tourism rather than terrorism requires some mental calisthenics.

(5) Northern Ireland _____ the northeastern portion of the island of Ireland.

(6) This is where you'll find the Botanic Gardens, art galleries, and museums, _____ a buzzing nightlife scene.

(7) It's easiest to start in the center and then _____ from there.
(8) In a 2005 poll, the Giant's Causeway _____ the fourth greatest natural wonder in the United Kingdom.

2. **Fill in the blanks with the appropriate form of the words in the brackets.**
   (1) Northern Ireland is considered an _____ (integrality) part of the United Kingdom.
   (2) The _____ (measure) of the island are 174 miles in _____ (wide), and 302 miles in _____ (long).
   (3) The shorelines of NI are characterized by many _____ (irregular).
   (4) For its small area, NI has a great _____ (vary) of _____ (scene) countryside.
   (5) This _____ (designate) is designed to protect and enhance the qualities of each area and to _____ (promotion) their _____ (enjoy) by the public.
   (6) Being the most _____ (industrialize) part of the island, NI supports one-third of the island's total population.
   (7) NI is still the poorest part of the United Kingdom. In 1986, Northern Ireland had a high _____ (employ) rate of around 21 percent.
   (8) There are three newspapers in NI: Belfast Telegraph, Irish News, and News Letter. _____ (combine) _____ (circulate) is about 272,000.
   (9) Due to this, Belfast was the target of several _____ (destroy) air raids during WWII.
   (10) It was a _____ (land) place for United States forces. It has very valuable key agricultural and industrial resources of the province. This is why NI is of such _____ (strategy) _____ (important).
   (11) For those who grew up in the 1970s and 1980s when Belfast was plagued by _____ (violent) and political _____ (rest), to think of it now in terms of _____ (tourist) rather than _____ (terrorist) requires some _____ (mentality) calisthenics.
   (12) You really see little sign of any _____ (residue) religious tension in the city center.
   (13) It is a pleasure to wander its pedestrianized lanes, to shop in the upscale arcades _____ (line) with _____ (glitter) jewelry stores and colorful boutiques, to linger in the historic pubs and to _____ (dinner) in the Michelin-starred restaurants.
   (14) The _____ (sect) areas, with the famous I.R.A. and Protestant murals, are just to the west of the city center.

3. **Fill in the blanks with the proper prepositions and adverbs that collocate with the neighboring words.**
   (1) The shorelines of Northern Ireland are characterized _____ many irregularities.
   (2) The tops of the columns of the Giant's Causeway form stepping stones that lead _____ the cliff foot and disappear _____ the sea.

(3) Most of the columns are hexagonal, although there are also some _____ four, five, seven and eight sides.
(4) In recent years, the center has been polished _____.
(5) Because this is an extraordinary time to visit this city, as it is still in the process of picking itself _____ and dusting itself _____ after years of strife.
(6) This is the best place for shopping, particularly _____ Donegall Place, which extends north from the square, _____ Royal Avenue. Bedford Street which travels south _____ the Donegall Square, becomes Dublin Road, which, in turn, leads south _____ the University Quarter, the leafy area _____ Queen's University.
(7) This is why NI is _____ such strategic importance.
(8) Motorways and railways transport people and goods _____ the country.

4. **Translate into English the following sentences with "it" as the preparatory subject.**
(1) It is a pleasure to wander its pedestrianized lanes.
(2) It is easiest to start in the center and then branch out from there.
(3) It's no use studying for an exam at the last minute.
(4) It doesn't make any difference my being there.
(5) It is a bore having to go out on a cold night like this.
(6) It is well-known that Edison invented the electric bulb.
(7) It is amazing that she should have said nothing about the murder.
(8) It is appropriate that he (should) be present.

Comprehensive Work

1. **Pair Work:** Locate the following on the map of Northern Island, and discuss their importance with your partner:
the Atlantic Ocean
the North Channel
the Irish Sea
Lough Neagh
Belfast
the Mourn Mountains

2. **Solo Work:** What is the following cartoon about? Do you know leprechauns in Irish folklore? Search some information about it and share your understanding of the cartoon with your classmates.

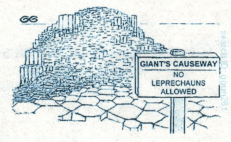

3. Solo Work: Write a brief introduction to Belfast, capital of Northern Ireland. It should include its location, population, city center, places to go, things to do, and its industry. Try to finish it within 300 words.

Read More

Text B　Legend of Giant's Causeway

Read the passage quickly and try to find the answer to the following questions.

1. Who built the Causeway? And why?
2. Why did his Scottish counterpart flee home in terror?

Legend has it that the Irish warrior Fionn mac Cumhaill (Finn McCool) built the causeway to walk to Scotland to fight his Scottish **counterpart** Benandonner. One version of the legend tells that Fionn fell asleep before he got to Scotland. When he did not arrive, the much larger Benandonner crossed the bridge looking for him. To protect Fionn, his wife Oonagh laid a blanket over him so he could pretend that he was actually their baby son. In a **variation**, Fionn fled after seeing Benandonner's great bulk, and asked his wife to disguise him as the baby. In both versions, when Benandonner saw the size of the "infant", he assumed the alleged father, Fionn, must be gigantic indeed. Therefore, Benandonner fled home in terror, **ripping up** the Causeway in case he was followed by Fionn.

Another variation is that Oonagh painted a rock shaped like a steak and gave it to Benandonner, whilst giving the baby (Fionn) a normal steak. When Benandonner saw that the baby was able to eat it so easily, he ran away, tearing up the causeway.

Text C　St. Patrick's Day

Write T in the brackets if the statement is true and write F if it is false.

1. Saint Patrick's Day is a particularly important day for Irish people and in Ireland. (　)

2. Patrick returned to Ireland to convert people to Buddism. ( )
3. People celebrate the holiday by wearing blue ribbons now. ( )
4. Patrick used the shamrock to explain the Holy Trinity to the pre-Christian Irish. ( )

Saint Patrick's Day is a particularly important day for Irish people and in Ireland. St. Patrick is the patron saint of Ireland. History says he was born in the year 387—so a long long time ago. **Apparently** he was taken slave in Ireland when he was a teenager but he escaped after a few years. He then later returned to Ireland to tell people about Jesus Christ and basically that is why he is seen as an important person.

These days St. Patrick's Day is basically a celebration of all things Irish. It is celebrated by Irish people, people who have connections to Ireland and non-Irish people around the world.

People generally celebrate by drinking—which is a traditional Irish way of celebrating—and probably drinking Guinness which is a traditional Irish drink. This is basically a dark and thick and strong tasting beer.

Green ribbons and shamrocks were worn in celebration of St. Patrick's Day as early as the 17th century, even though St. Patrick's Blue was the colour traditionally associated with St. Patrick. He is said to have used the shamrock, a three-leaved plant, to explain the Holy Trinity to the pre-Christian Irish, and the wearing and display of shamrocks and shamrock-inspired designs have become a **ubiquitous**  feature of the day. The phrase "the wearing of the green", meaning to wear a shamrock on one's clothing, **derives from** the song of the same name.

They might also eat traditional Irish food like stews and listen to traditional Irish music.

It is a public holiday in Ireland—lots of people go to church too on this day. But in Britain lots of people just celebrate it in the evening. There are parades in London and in fact all around the world.

Proper Nouns

Bedford Street 贝德福德大街
Belfast 贝尔法斯特
Belfast Telegraph 贝尔法斯特电讯报
Bradbury Place 布莱德伯里购物街
Donegall Place 登内格尔购物街
Donegall Square 登内格尔广场
Donegall Street 登内格尔大街
Dublin Road 都柏林大道
Great Victoria Street 维多利亚大街
I.R.A. (Irish Republican Army) 爱尔兰共和军

Irish News《爱尔兰新闻报》
News Letter《新闻通讯报》
Queen's University (of Belfast) 贝尔法斯特皇后大学
Radio Times《广播时代》杂志
Royal Avenue 皇家大道
Slieve Donard 多纳德山
St. Patricks Day 圣帕特里克节
the Black Cab 黑色出租车
the Cathedral Quarter 教堂区
the Falls road 福尔斯路
the Giant's Causeway 巨人之路
the Golden Mile 金域
the Holy Trinity (基督教)圣三一(指圣父、圣子、圣灵三位一体)
the Mourne Mountains 莫恩山脉
the Seat of Government 政府所在地
the Shankill road 香吉尔路
the University Quarter 大学区
Ulster 阿尔斯特
UNESCO 教科文组织

For Fun

Websites to visit

http://en.wikipedia.org/wiki/Northern_Ireland

　　This is a webpage about Northern Ireland, on which you can find information on its history, geography, economy, transport, culture, governance, education, law etc.

http://en.wikipedia.org/wiki/Belfast

　　This is a webpage about Belfast, on which you can find information on its history, governance, geography, demography, economy, architecture, culture, education etc.

Books to read

Belfast and Northern Ireland by Sean Sheehan, Pat Levy

　　It showcases a new Northern Ireland, safer now and fueled by a fresh energy, introducing readers to the many aspects of this much-misunderstood destination, increasingly a tourist mecca as big money has poured in. The book guides tourists through old and new Northern Ireland, from the stately 19th-century architecture that memorializes a rich history to the daring steel-and-glass ambience of the contemporary scene.

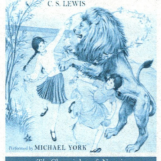

The Chronicles of Narnia by C. S. Lewis

　　It is a series of seven fantasy novels for children written by C.S. Lewis, who was born in Belfast, Northern Ireland in 1898. It is considered a classic of children's literature. They have been adapted several times, complete or in part, for radio, television, stage, and cinema. In addition to numerous traditional Christian themes, the series borrows characters and ideas from Greek and Roman mythology, as well as from traditional British and Irish fairy tales.

The Chronicles of Narnia present the adventures of children who play central roles in the unfolding history of the fictional realm of Narnia, a place where animals talk, magic is common, and good battles evil. Each of the books (with the exception of *The Horse and His Boy*) features as its protagonists children from our world who are magically transported to Narnia, where they are called upon to help the Lion Aslan handle a crisis in the world of Narnia.

Movies to see

Michael Collins(1996)

It is a 1996 historical biopic about General Michael Collins, the Irish patriot and revolutionary who died in the Irish Civil War. Neil Jordan depicts the controversial life and death of Michael Collins, the "Lion of Ireland", who led the IRA against British rule and founded the Irish Free State (Eire) in 1921. The film won the Golden Lion at the Venice Film Festival.

The Wind that Shakes the Barley(2006)

Ireland 1920: workers from field and country unite to form volunteer guerrilla armies to face the ruthless "Black and Tan" squads that are being shipped from Britain to block Ireland's bid for independence. Driven by a deep sense of duty and a love for his country, Damien abandons his burgeoning career as a doctor and joins his brother, Teddy, in a dangerous and violent fight for freedom. As the freedom fighters' bold tactics bring the British to breaking point, both sides finally agree to a treaty to end the bloodshed. But, despite the apparent victory, civil war erupts and families, who fought side by side, find themselves pitted against one another as sworn enemies, putting their loyalties to the ultimate test.

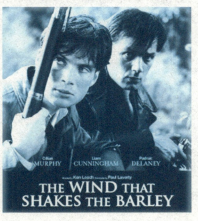

Song to enjoy

<u>The Wearing of the Green</u>

It is an anonymously-penned Irish street ballad dating to 1798. The context of the song is the repression around the time of the Irish Rebellion of 1798. Wearing a shamrock in the "caubeen" (hat) was a sign of rebellion and green was the colour of the Society of the United Irishmen, a republican revolutionary organisation.

O Paddy dear, and did ye hear the news that's goin' round?
The shamrock is by law forbid to grow on Irish ground!
No more Saint Patrick's Day we'll keep, his color can't be seen
For there's a cruel law ag'in the Wearin' o' the Green.

I met with Napper Tandy, and he took me by the hand,
And he said, "How's poor old Ireland, and how does she stand?"
"She's the most distressful country that ever yet was seen,
For they're hanging men and women there for the Wearin' o' the Green."

"So if the color we must wear be England's cruel red
Let it remind us of the blood that Irishmen have shed;
And pull the shamrock from your hat, and throw it on the sod
But never fear, 'twill take root there, though underfoot' tis trod.

When laws can stop the blades of grass from growin' as they grow
And when the leaves in summer-time their color dare not show,
Then I will change the color too I wear in my caubeen;
But till that day, please God, I'll stick to the Wearin' o' the Green."

Unit 15

Review of the UK

> Britannia rule the waves. Britons never, never, never shall be slaves.
>
> —James Thomson

Unit Goals

- To have a summary about the UK
- To reinforce the useful geographical terms about the UK
- To learn the useful words and expressions that describe the regional differences in the UK and improve English language skills

Before You Read

Which country is the statement about, England, Wales, Scotland or Northern Island?

1. It is in north-west Europe and is in the southern part of Great Britain. _____
2. It is located on a peninsula in central-west Great Britain. _____
3. It occupies a third of the islands of Great Britain. _____
4. The people of this country liked thistle so much that they made it their national flower. _____
5. It is situated in the northeastern portion of the island of Ireland. _____
6. It consists of mountains surrounding Lough Neagh on its northwest, northeast, and southeast. _____

7. It is only 35 km from France and is now linked by a tunnel under the English Channel. _____
8. Much of its diverse landscape is mountainous, particularly in the north and central regions. _____

Start to Read

Text A Review of England and Scotland

Review of the Nine Regions of England

A journey through England is a journey through history—from the ancient megaliths of Stonehenge to the space-age domes of the Eden Project in Cornwall. It is also a trip to the 21st century: London is **gearing up** for the 2012 Olympics while cities like Manchester, Leeds and Newcastle **revel** in their heritage and confidently face the future, with industrial buildings **revitalised** as waterfront galleries or trendy apartments, flanked by **tempting** bars, shops, restaurants and some of the finest music venues in the world.

1. **South West:** This region has one coast on the Channel and one on the Bristol Channel. It includes such popular destinations as the proud county of Cornwall, Devon and its Jurassic Coast, Somerset with places such as Cheddar and the County Town of Taunton, Dorset—Thomas Hardy country, the Roman Baths, and American Museum in Bath inspiringly in Bath and North East Somerset. It is also home to parts of the Cotswolds.

2. **South East:** With distinctive castles and a coastline on the English Channel, the South East of England is a leading region in tourism outside of London. Among the many popular destinations here are charming Cotswolds, renowned Canterbury, Oxford and its colleges and universities and the Thames River.

3. **London:** Filled with famous sights and attractions like the Big Ben, the Tower of London, the Tower Bridge, Buckingham Palace and Trafalgar Square, London is today a center of international finance, world-class education and global politics. At its peak in the 19th century, London was as great as Rome in the age of Caesar. Tourists can **catch a glimpse of** the United

Kingdom's glorious imperial history in the Imperial War Museum and the National Gallery.

 4. East of England: It is home to the Counties of Essex, Suffolk, Norfolk and Cambridgeshire. Among the many attractions are the world-renowned University of Cambridge, **well-preserved** and visually impressive Norwich Cathedral.

 5. East Midlands: The East Midlands has a coastline on the North Sea and Includes the towns of Nottingham, Derby and Leicester. Pay a visit to Nottingham Castle, Calke Abbey and Bosworth Battlefield, all attractions located in this region of England.

 6. West Midlands: It is home to Birmingham, England's second largest city, Birthplace of Cadbury's chocolate and Ozzy Osborne. It is also home to Coventry, England's ninth largest city, the home of Lady Godiva (after whom the famous line of chocolate is named) and once the center of British automobile manufacturing.

 7. North West: It is considered the beating heart of England, both geographically and culturally, and it is best known for its two world class cities, Liverpool and Manchester. The influence of the North West on science and technology, politics, sport and media is **undeniable**. The Industrial Revolution started here. It is the home of many world renowned band—The Beatles, Oasis, New Order, Joy Division to name but a few. In sport both Manchester United and Liverpool FC are based in the North West. Also **of note** in the North West are Cumbria and its Lake District, known as one of the most scenic areas of the UK.

 8. Yorkshire and the Humber: Among the most traveled-to cities here are Leeds, York and Sheffield. Don't miss York Minster, the National Railway Museum or the Leeds United F.C. Stadium.

 9. North East: The most popular destination here is the city of Newcastle-upon-Tyne, which boasts a well-preserved Norman castle built under King Henry II in the 12th century and is the **namesake** of Newcastle Brown Ale, served in pubs around the world.

Review of Scotland

 Scotland forms the northern part of the island of Great Britain. It is 31, 510 square miles in area; it is 274 miles long from North to South and varies in **breadth** between 24 and 154 miles.

 The official language is English, although Gaelic is spoken, primarily in the North and West of Scotland. The Scots language (which has many similarities to English, but also draws on French and Gaelic) is also spoken. Whereas Gaelic is the language of the Highlands and Islands, Scots is the language of the Lowlands.

The national flower is the thistle, although the heather which covers significant moorland areas is also closely associated with the country, providing peat for the fire and, along with lichens, dyes for tartan.

Scotland is divided into three main regions: the Highlands, the Midland Valley (the Central Lowland) and the Southern Uplands. The cities of Edinburgh, Glasgow and Dundee together with numerous towns, most of the population and the majority of Scotland's industry are located within the Midland Valley (the central lowland). It is geologically distinct from the surrounding regions, being composed of Devonian Old Red Sandstone, **peppered with** ancient volcanoes, as against the older sedimentary rocks forming the Southern Uplands or the ancient metamorphic melange, comprising the Highlands to the north.

Scotland includes 787 islands, of which most belong to groups known as the Hebrides, Orkney and Shetland. Only 62 exceed three square miles in area.

Of 26 rivers flowing directly into the sea, the Rivers Clyde, Forth and Tay open into significant estuaries and support three of the major cities of Scotland (Glasgow, Edinburgh and Dundee respectively).

Scotland is well known for its mountainous and beautiful scenery. Much of the upland within the UK is contained within the borders of Scotland, along with the highest peaks.

Scotland is also noted for its lochs (this name is generally used for lakes in Scotland). Much of the west coast of the country is **intersected** by Sea Lochs, the longest of which, Loch Fyne, **penetrates** more than 40 miles inland. Notable fresh-water lochs include Loch Ness (the one with the Monster!).

After You Read

Knowledge Focus

1. **Fill in the blanks according to the geographical knowledge you have learned in the text above.**

    (1) A journey through _____ is a journey through history—from the ancient megaliths of Stonehenge to the space-age domes of the Eden Project in Cornwall.

    (2) _____ west is home to parts of the Cotswolds.

    (3) With distinctive castles and a coastline on the English Channel, _____ of

England is a leading region in tourism outside of London.

(4) At its peak in the 19th century, _____ was as great as Rome in the age of Caesar.

(5) The _____ has a coastline on the North Sea and include the towns of Nottingham, Derby and Leicester.

(6) _____ is home to Birmingham, England's second largest city, Birthplace of Cadbury's chocolate and Ozzy Osborne.

(7) _____ forms the northern part of the island of Great Britain.

(8) Most of the population and the majority of Scotland's industry are located within the _____.

2. **Write T in the brackets if the statement is true and write F if it is false.**

(1) Among the many popular destinations, South East has charming Cotswolds, renowned Canterbury, Oxford and its colleges and universities and the Thames River. (　)

(2) In London, tourists can catch a glimpse of the United Kingdom's glorious imperial history in the Imperial War Museum and the National Gallery. (　)

(3) Among the many attractions of South East are the world-renowned University of Cambridge, well-preserved and visually impressive Norwich Cathedral. (　)

(4) North West is considered the beating heart of England, both geographically and culturally, and it is best known for its two world class cities, Liverpool and Manchester. (　)

(5) The Industrial Revolution started from North East. (　)

(6) The official language in the North and West of Scotland is Gaelic. (　)

(7) The national flower of Scotland is the thistle. (　)

(8) Scotland is well known for its mountainous and beautiful scenery. (　)

Language Focus

1. **Fill in the blanks with the proper form of the phrases below.**

be filled with	draw on	be gearing up for
be distinct from	pay a visit to	at one's peak
be associated with	be divided into	

(1) It is also a trip to the 21st century: London _____ the 2012 Olympics.

(2) It is worthwhile to _____ Nottingham Castle, Calke Abbey and Bosworth Battlefield, all attractions located in this region of England.

(3) The national flower of Scotland is the thistle, although the heather which covers significant moorland areas _____ the country.

(4) Scotland _____ three main regions: the Highlands, the Midland Valley and the Southern Uplands.

(5) The Scots language (which has many similarities to English, but also _____ French and Gaelic) is also spoken.

(6) London _____ famous sights and attractions like the Big Ben, the Tower of

London, the Tower Bridge, Buckingham Palace and Trafalgar Square.

(7) It _____ the surrounding regions, being composed of Devonian Old Red Sandstone, peppered with ancient volcanoes.

(8) _____ in the 19th century, London was as great as Rome in the age of Caesar.

2. **Fill in the blanks with the appropriate form of the words in the brackets.**

(1) With _____ (distinct) castles and a coastline on the English Channel, the South East of England is a leading region in tourism outside of London.

(2) _____ (tour) can catch a glimpse of the United Kingdom's glorious imperial history in the Imperial War Museum and the National Gallery.

(3) Among the many attractions are the world-renowned University of Cambridge, well-preserved and visually _____ (impression) Norwich Cathedral.

(4) It is home to Birmingham, England's second _____ (large) city, Birthplace of Cadbury's chocolate and Ozzy Osborne.

(5) It is considered the _____ (beat) heart of England, both geographically and culturally, and it is best known for its two world class cities, Liverpool and Manchester.

(6) Cumbria and its Lake District are known as one of the most _____ (scene) areas of the UK.

(7) The most popular destination here is the city of Newcastle-upon-Tyne, which boasts a well-preserved Norman castle _____ (build) under King Henry II in the 12th century and is the namesake of Newcastle Brown Ale, served in pubs around the world.

(8) The official language is English, although Gaelic is spoken, _____ (primary) in the North and West of Scotland.

(9) It is geologically distinct from the _____ (surround) regions.

(10) _____ (note) fresh-water lochs include Loch Ness (the one with the Monster!).

3. **Fill in the blanks with the proper prepositions and adverbs that collocate with the neighboring words.**

(1) A journey through England is a journey _____ history—from the ancient megaliths of Stonehenge to the space-age domes of the Eden Project in Cornwall.

(2) The influence of the North West _____ science and technology, politics, sport and media is undeniable.

(3) It is also home to Coventry, England's ninth largest city, the home of Lady Godiva _____ whom the famous line of chocolate is named and once the center of British automobile manufacturing.

(4) Both Manchester united and Liverpool FC are based _____ the North East.

(5) The most popular destination here is the city of Newcastle-upon-Tyne, which boasts a well-preserved Norman castle built _____ King Henry II in the 12th century.

(6) The national flower is the thistle, although the heather which covers significant

moorland areas is also closely associated with the country, providing peat _____ the fire and, along _____ lichens, dyes _____ tartan.

(7) Scotland includes 787 islands, _____ which most belong to groups known as the Hebrides, Orkney and Shetland.

(8) The Rivers Clyde, Forth and Tay open _____ significant estuaries and support three of the major cities of Scotland.

Comprehensive Work

1. **Solo Work:** Locate the nine regions of England on the following map.

2. **Pair Work:** Discuss, with your partner, which region in England is most impressive in your eye? And why? Take down your partner's view and then share it with your neighbours.

   The best region _____

   The reason(s) _____
   _____
   _____

3. **Group Work:** If you are in London and are going to Edinburgh, which towns and cities would you visit on the way? And for what? Share your opinion in groups of three or four students.

   From London to Newcastle

Towns to be visited	Reasons
_____	_____
_____	_____
_____	_____

4. **Solo Work:** Write a composition of about 300 words on the region you want to visit most in England and tell your readers why.

Read More

Text B — Review of Wales

Read the passage quickly and match the possible meaning of the underlined words.

(1) hilly   a. flourishing
(2) thriving   b. density
(3) currently   c. mountainous
(4) concentration d. presently

Wales is the friendly green <u>hilly</u> bit on the western side of Britain. It is about 2 hours west of London by rail or by road.

It might not take you long to get here, but you'll find that Wales is a very different place.

First there is the language: it is one of the oldest in Europe, spoken fluently by about one in five of the population. Although people all speak English as well, Welsh is a <u>thriving</u> mainstay of ways of life.

Then there is the landscape. The facts and figures might lead you to believe that Wales is small—it covers an area of around 8,000 square miles (or 20,800 square kilometres). But if you could roll it out flat, we bet it would be bigger than Texas.

There are 3 National Parks and 5 Areas of Outstanding Natural Beauty, all part of a landscape that offers opportunities for all kinds of activities. Walking, cycling, climbing, golf, mountain biking and paragliding are just the beginning of the list.

The population <u>currently</u> stands at around 3 million people, so there's plenty of room.

There are also lots and lots of castles (over 400 at the last count), the Welsh National Opera (one of the world's premier Opera Companies), the largest single-span glasshouse in the world (at the National Botanic Garden of Wales), and a cool flag with a Red Dragon on it.

The capital city is Cardiff. The Romans had a fortress here in the first Century A.D., but Cardiff's a lively youngster really. It was officially designated as capital in 1955, and it is home to a large <u>concentration</u> of media and creative types, turning out award-winning productions like the current incarnation of the legendary Dr Who series.

Text C Review of Northern Ireland

Read the passage quickly and try to find the information to fill in the blanks below.

(1) Occupying the northeastern corner of an island brimming with superlatives, _____ contains many hidden facets of the Emerald Isle.

(2) The capital, _____, is a vibrant city with ornate Victorian architecture and lively nightlife.

(3) The _____ is one of the most scenic shorelines in Britain, winding past towering cliffs, sandy beaches, picturesque harbours and family resorts.

(4) Inland lies _____, the largest lake in the British Isles, and the Fermanagh lakelands, sprinkled with tiny islands, wooded parks and monastic ruins.

Occupying the northeastern corner of an island **brimming** with superlatives, Northern Ireland contains many hidden facets of the Emerald Isle. This small province enjoys a diverse terrain with a **dramatic** coastline, gently rolling fields and the **lush** Mountains of Mourne. The capital, Belfast, is a vibrant city with **ornate** Victorian architecture and lively nightlife. Londonderry is one of the finest walled towns in Europe. Both have been too long **overshadowed** by the "Troubles", but seem at last to be enjoying a more peaceful present.

The Antrim Coast is one of the most scenic shorelines in Britain, winding past towering cliffs, sandy beaches, picturesque harbours and family resorts. You can hike deep into the glacier-carved Glens of Antrim or walk along the amazing volcanic columns of the Giant's Causeway. Inland lies Lough Neagh, the largest lake in the British Isles, and the Fermanagh lakelands, **sprinkled with** tiny islands, wooded parks and monastic ruins.

The six counties of Northern Ireland belonged to the ancient and powerful kingdom of Ulster. Tales of legendary heroes **intertwine with** those of St. Patrick, who spread Christianity from his base near Downpatrick. The Ulster American Folk Park near Omagh, Old Bushmill's whiskey distillery, the Belleek pottery, crumbling castle ruins and the stately mansions of the Anglo-Irish aristocracy offer more history and culture in a friendly, **easy-going** country that is a delight to explore.

Proper Nouns

Bosworth Battlefield 波斯沃斯战场　　　　　Calke Abbey 卡尔克修道院
Cadbury's chocolate 吉百利巧克力　　　　　Devonian 泥盆纪(古代生物的一个时期)的

Downpatrick 唐帕特里克镇
Dr Who《神秘博士》(英剧)
Dundee 敦提
Glens of Antrim 安特里姆峡谷
Joy Division 快乐小分队乐队
King Henry II 亨利二世
Liverpool FC 利物浦足球俱乐部
Loch Fyne 落奇菲湖
Londonderry 伦敦德里
Manchester United 曼彻斯特联队
Newcastle Brown Ale 纽卡斯尔棕色淡啤酒
New Order 新秩序乐队
Norman castle 诺曼底城堡
Nottingham Castle 诺丁汉城堡
Oasis 绿洲乐队
Old Bushmill 老布什米尔(爱尔兰威士忌酒)
Old Red Sandstone 老红砂岩
Omagh 奥马
Ozzy Osborne 奥兹·奥斯本(乐队吉他手)
Sheffield 设菲尔德
the Antrim Coast 安特里姆海岸
the age of Caesar 凯撒时代
the Belleek pottery 伯利克陶瓷皿
the County Town of Taunton 陶顿郡
the Eden Project 伊甸生态园区
the Emerald Isle 绿宝石岛(爱尔兰的别称)
the Fermanagh lakelands 弗马纳郡湖泊地区
the Imperial War Museum 帝国战争博物馆
the Industrial Revolution 工业革命
the Leeds United F. C. Stadium 利兹足球俱乐部看台
the National Botanic Garden of Wales 威尔士国家植物园
the National Gallery 国家美术馆
the National Railway Museum 国家铁路博物馆
the Ulster American Folk Park 阿尔斯特美国民俗公园
the Welsh National Opera 威尔士国家歌剧院
Thomas Hardy 托马斯·哈代(英国诗人、小说家)

For Fun

Websites to visit

For more information on England, visit：http://www.england.com/
For more information on Scotland, visit：http://www.scotland.com/
For more information on Wales, visit：http://www.wales.com/
For more information on Northern Ireland, visit：
http://www.discovernorthernireland.com/

Book to read

1000 Things to Do in Britain by Times Out Guide Ltd.

The features include castles and kayaking, sculpture gardens and snorkelling hotspots, white sand beaches and white-knuckle rides, cider orchards and stately homes. Covering the length and breadth of Britain, it takes in both life-changing experiences and simple pleasures, with ideas for every budget. You can go wild camping on Dartmoor, or be pampered in a luxury spa; forage for your supper, or take afternoon tea in Park Lane; ride along a deserted beach, or go wild in the crowd at a festival.

Movie to see
Battle of Britain（1969）

It is a historical reenactment of the air war in the early days of World War Two for control of the skies over Britain as the new Luftwaffa and the Royal Air Force determine whether or not an invasion can take place.

Song to enjoy
Rule, Britannia!

It is a British patriotic song, originating from the poem "Rule, Britannia" by James Thomson and set to music by Thomas Arne in 1740.

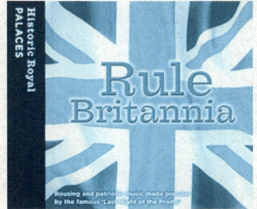

When Britain first, at heaven's command,
Arose from out the azure main,
Arose, arose, arose from out the azure main,
This was the charter, the charter of the land,
And guardian angels sang this strain:

Rule Britania!
Britannia rule the waves.
Britons never, never, never shall be slaves.

Rule Britannia!
Britannia rule the waves.
Britons never, never, never shall be slaves.

The nations, not so blest as thee,
Must in their turn, to tyrants fall,
Must in, must in, must in their turn, to tyrants fall,
While thou shalt flourish, shalt flourish great and free,
The dread and envy of them all.
(Chorus)
Rule Britannia!
Britannia rule the waves.
Britons never, never, never shall be slaves.

Rule Britannia!
Britannia rule the waves.
Brittons never, never, never shall be slaves.

Appendixes

Appendix 1 Symbols of Constituent Countries of the UK

Country	Patron Saint	National Flower(s)	National Animal(s)	Motto	Anthem
England	St. George	Tudor Rose	Lion	Dieu et mon droit (French) "God and my right"	Currently, no official national Anthem specifically for England
Northern Ireland	St. Patrick	Shamrock or Flax	—	None formerly Quis separabit? (Latin) "Who will separate?" [citation needed]	"Londonderry Air"
Scotland	St. Andrew	Thistle	Unicorn	In My Defens God Me Defend (Scots)	Flower of Scotland
Wales	St. David	Leek or Daffodil	Red Dragon	Cymru am byth (Welsh) "Wales forever"	"Hen Wlad Fy Nhadau" (Welsh) Land of my Fathers

Appendix 2 National Flags

Flag	Date	Use	Description	Status
	1801 –	The Union Flag, popularly known as the Union Jack. Used as the flag of the United Kingdom	A superimposition of the flags of England and Scotland with the Saint Patrick's Saltire (representing Ireland)	National flag used by government
	c. 1275 –	Flag of England, also known as the St George's Cross	A red cross on a white field	De facto national flag used mainly by the Church of England
	c. 1300 –	Flag of Scotland, also known as the St Andrew's Cross, or the Saltire	A white saltire on a blue field	National flag used by Scottish Government and agencies, as well as by ordinary citizens.
	1959 –	Flag of Wales, also known as the Red Dragon or Y Ddraig Goch	A red passant dragon on a green and white field	De facto national flag used by the Welsh Assembly Government and agencies

重点参考书目和网站

Britannica: http://www.britannica.com/EBchecked/topic/236663/God-Save-the-Queen
Campbell, Donald Grant. *Scotland in Pictures*. Lerner Publishing Group, 1991.
Carter, Harold. *An Urban Geography of England and Wales in the Nineteenth Century*. Edward Arnold, 1992.
Cunningham, Sophie. *Geography*. Transworld Publishers, 2005.
Dodgshon, Robert A. *Historical Geography of England and Wales*. Academic Press, 1991.
Dorling, Danny. *Human Geography of the UK*. Sage Publications Ltd., 2005.
England Background: http://www.tripadvisor.com/Travel-g186217-s2/England: United-Kingdom: Background.html
Explore the Travel Guides: http://travel.yahoo.com/p-travelguide
Family Attractions in London: http://www.visitlondon.com/people/family/
Fielding, Penny. *Scotland and the Fictions of Geography: North Britain 1760-1830*. Cambridge University Press, 2009.
Frommers Travel Guide: http://www.frommers.com
Gardiner, Vince. *Changing Geography of the UK*. Routledge, 1999.
Graham, David. *Human Geography of the UK: An Introduction*. Routledge, 2001.
Hotel and Beach Resorts: http://www.southtravels.com
Ireland, Free family Crests. Maps, Genealogy and Information: http://www.ireland-information.com/irishmusic/thewearingofthegreen.shtml
Know Britain: http://www.know-britain.com
London Landmarks and London Monuments: http://www.london.world-guides.com.html
Lonely Planet Travel Guides and Travel Information: http://www.lonelyplanet.com
Lowson, Nigel. *A New Geography of Wales*. Cambridge University Press, 1992.
Lyrics: http://www.metrolyrics.com
Manchester & the North West Region of England: http://www.manchester2002-uk.com
Mp3lyrics: http://www.mp3lyrics.org/b/beatles/love-me-do/
Nach, James. *England in Pictures*. Lerner Publishing Group, 1990.
Nagle, Garrett. *Britain's Changing Environment*. Nelson Thornes Ltd., 1999.
North East Letting: http://www.northeastlettings.com/tenantinfo/newcastle.htm
Northern Ireland Overview: http://www.iexplore.com/dmap/Northern+Ireland/Overview
Nottingham: http://www.visitnottingham.com
Polley, Derek. *Home Ground: Foundation Level: A Geography of Northern Ireland*. Colourpoint Books, 2002.
Rampant Scotland Directory: http://www.rampantscotland.com
Roots Web.com: http://www.rootsweb.ancestry.com
Scotland Geography: http://library.thinkquest.org/J0112187/scotland_geography.htm
Search Any Lyrics: http://www.searchanylyrics.com
Some Facts and Figures about Wales: http://www.data-wales.co.uk/wstats.htm
South East of England: http://www.visitsoutheastengland.com
Stonehenge and Avebury, England: http://www.terragalleria.com/europe/united-kingdom/

stonehenge-avebury/stonehenge-avebury.html

The Beatles：http://www.thebeatles.com/core/home/

The Complete Free Lyrics Database：http://www.lyricspy.com

The Future for Bath and North East Somerset：http://www.bathnes.gov.uk/future/Bath/Identity＋and＋Vision/The＋soul＋of＋Bath.htm

The Gateway to Scotland：http://www.geo.ed.ac.uk/home/scotland/scotland.html

The Geography of Wales：http://www.bbc.co.uk/wales/culture/sites/aboutwales/pages/geography.shtml

The Internet Movie Database：http://www.imdb.com

Unesco，World Heritage Centre：http://whc.unesco.org/en/list/373

Visit East of England：http://www.visiteastofengland.com

Visit Lincolnshire：http://www.visitlincolnshire.com

Visit Wales UK：http://www.canada.visitwales.com/server.php?show＝nav.3565

Wales History：http://www.suite101.com/article.cfm/wales_history/91713

Wales，Lands of Celts and Mountains，Lakes and Woodlands：http://www.stayinbritain.co.uk/country/wales.aspx

Wikipedia, the Free Encyclopedia：http://en.wikipedia.org/wiki

World Atlas：http://www.worldatlas.com

David Else. 英国(旅行指南系列). 北京：三联书店，2007.

M.D.M. 麦肯齐. 英国背景. 北京：世界图书出版公司，1995.

北京大陆桥文化传媒. 英国往事. 重庆：重庆出版社，2007.

韩晓惠，周华. A Survey of Great Britain. 哈尔滨：哈尔滨工业大学出版社，2005.

何田. 英语学习背景知识(英国澳大利亚). 北京：北京大学出版社，2001.

亨利·詹姆斯著. 英国风情. 思齐译. 北京：东方出版社，2005.

黄铁聚. 英国(世界通览). 哈尔滨：哈尔滨工程大学出版社，2004.

金良浚. 英国(世界之旅). 北京：旅游教育出版社，2000.

克里斯托弗·萨默维尔. 英国. 赵志恒等译. 沈阳：辽宁教育出版社，2002.

孔翔兰，赵东林. 西方文化风情路——英国篇. 西安：西北工业大学出版社，2007.

李念培，孙正达. 英国(世界列国国情习俗丛书). 北京：当代世界出版社 1998.

李秀杰. 英国(目击者旅游指南). 北京：中国旅游出版社，2008.

王振华. 英国(列国志). 北京：社会科学文献出版社，2003.

张玉钧，刘东妮，王姗姗. 英国(走遍全球). 北京：中国旅游出版社，2007.

《英国国情:英国自然人文地理》

尊敬的老师:

您好!

为了方便您更好地使用本教材,获得最佳教学效果,我们特向使用该书作为教材的教师赠送本教材配套课件资料。如有需要,请完整填写"教师联系表"并加盖所在单位系(院)公章,免费向出版社索取。

北京大学出版社

教 师 联 系 表

教材名称	《英国国情:英国自然人文地理》			
姓名:	性别:	职务:		职称:
E-mail:	联系电话:		邮政编码:	
供职学校:	所在院系:			(章)
学校地址:				
教学科目与年级:	班级人数:			
通信地址:				

填写完毕后,请将此表邮寄给我们,我们将为您免费寄送本教材配套资料,谢谢!

北京市海淀区成府路205号
北京大学出版社外语编辑部　初艳红
邮政编码:100871
电子邮箱:alicechu2008@126.com

邮 购 部 电 话:010-62752015
市场营销部电话:010-62750672
外语编辑部电话:010-62759634